FIFTY PLACES TO TRAVEL WITH YOUR DOG

BEFORE YOU DIE

FIFTY PLACES TO

TRAVEL WITH YOUR DOG

BEFORE YOU DIE

**Dog Experts Share
the World's Greatest Destinations**

Chris Santella *and* DC Helmuth

FOREWORD BY MELISSA HALLIBURTON

ABRAMS IMAGE

NEW YORK

For my wife, Deidre, my daughters, Cassidy and Annabel, and our rescue dog, Lola *(Chris)*
For Robin and Gambit *(DC)*

Contents

ACKNOWLEDGMENTS

This book would not have been possible without the assistance of the dog lovers who shared their voices with us. To these people, we offer the most heartfelt thanks. We would also like to thank editors Samantha Weiner, Juliet Dore, and Annalea Manalili; designer Anna Christian; copy editor Ivy McFadden, and proofreader Sabina Friedman-Seitz who helped bring the book into being.

DC would like to offer special thanks to Danielle Svetcov and Chris Santella, for so warmly sharing the privilege of writing another volume in this special series. Special thanks to Justin Castilla and Joanna Robinson for help conducting interviews, and to Cindy Roberts, Kim Helmuth, and Jacole Helmuth for their ongoing support.

Chris would like to offer special thanks to his agent, Stephanie Rostan, and to his wife, Deidre, and daughters Cassidy and Annabel, for their patience and unwavering support. And to Lola, our rescue Chihuahua, who has brought us incredible joy since she entered our lives. As the saying goes, we didn't save her so much as she saved us!

OPPOSITE:
Two travelers celebrate the view of downtown Toronto.

9

FOREWORD

In March 2020, a figurative earthquake shook the foundation of the company I had poured fifteen years of my life into building. When the world locked down due to COVID-19, my focus at work suddenly shifted from planning road trips for people and pets to outlining a road map for the survival of my business. As the aftershocks reverberated in the days and weeks ahead, I spent countless hours pondering whether life would ever return to normal and many restless nights questioning when the world would begin traveling again.

With humanity shut in at home for months and the pace of life slowing, a curious thing happened: The bond between people and pets grew stronger. Frustrating commutes were replaced with relaxing neighborhood walks. Kennels were ditched in favor of snuggles. Millions of us adopted "pandemic puppies." Some even took up baking (my pups enjoyed freshly baked dog treats on more than one occasion). Slowly but surely, fear and angst gave way to wanderlust and a fierce yearning to hit the road again. And, this time, more than ever before, our dogs came along for the ride.

For most of my life, a furry copilot has accompanied me in my crazy travel adventures. My first dog, Rocco, inspired me to create BringFido, a first of its kind dog travel agency, and devote a career to making the world a more pet-friendly place. Over the past twenty years, I've made numerous friends and traveled far and wide on hundreds of adventures (many of which are found in this book) that simply would not have been possible without my dogs. We've schmoozed with celebrity pets, crowned dog surfing champions, slept in every accommodation type imaginable (including the world's largest beagle), and attended countless dog parades, fashion shows, yappy hours, and charitable events. My dog Ace has visited every state in the continental US, and his ears perk up every time he hears the words "road trip!"

If you live to travel but can't stand the thought of leaving behind your furry family members, *50 Places to Travel With Your Dog Before You Die* is a worthy read. Chris Santella and DC Helmuth, along with help from many colorful contributors, have compiled an indispensable resource for pet parents who love traveling alongside their four-legged friends. The book is an inspiration to anyone intrigued by the prospect of going on a pet-friendly adventure.

—MELISSA HALLIBURTON, CEO AND FOUNDER OF BRINGFIDO.COM

INTRODUCTION

DNA analysis suggests that the first of the mammals we now know as dogs began to appear 130,000 years ago—presumably as *some* wolves recognized the *potential* benefits that humans could provide. An occasional meal and shelter, for example, in exchange for the protection of a sharp fang and a smart bark—and, perhaps, a scratch behind the ears. Agricultural societies were still more than one hundred thousand years away, so our hunter-gatherer ancestors were constantly on the move. Their canid cohorts tagged along, at least some of the time. We can only conjecture how these ancient humans perceived their four-legged fellow travelers. As protectors? Freeloaders?

Or companions?

We certainly know how we'd answer that question today!

According to the American Veterinary Medical Association's *2017–2018 U.S. Pet Ownership and Demographics Sourcebook,* Americans keep nearly 77 million dogs as pets; that's at least one dog for 38 percent of the country's households. It's estimated that more than 100 hundred million Americans will travel more than 50 miles from home for a vacation each year; these days, over half will take Fido along. People are now weighing potential travel destinations not solely on criteria that will please them; they are taking their *dogs'* needs into consideration, too.

We wrote *Fifty Places to Travel with Your Dog Before You Die* to provide a road map and inspirational guide for those who would take Fido along wherever they go.

"What makes a place a good destination to travel with your dog before you die?" you might ask. A welcoming, inclusive attitude toward dogs, and a desire to treat them as part of the family? An abundance of dog-friendly hiking trails or swimming holes? A special setting created especially with dogs in mind? Or simply the chance to commune with other dog lovers? The answer would be yes to all of the above.

One thing we knew when we began this project: We were *NOT* the people to assemble this list. So we followed a recipe that worked well in the first seventeen Fifty Places books—we sought the advice of some committed dog travelers. To write *Fifty Places to Travel with Your Dog Before You Die,* we interviewed a host of people who have expert experience with dogs and travel and asked them to share some of their favorite destinations.

These experts range from noted dog travel specialists (like Melissa Halliburton of BringFido.com) to dog advocates (like Edward Flores) to employees of leading dog equipment companies (like Lanette Fidrych of Cycle Dog and Dani Reese of Ruffwear). Some spoke of venues that are near and dear to their hearts, places they call home; others spoke of places they've only visited once, but that made a profound impression. People and their dogs relate to place in many different ways, and we've done our best to reflect that diversity here. (To give a sense of the breadth of the interviewees' backgrounds, a bio of each individual is included after each essay.)

Satisfying dog travel can mean different things to different people (and dogs!). *Fifty Places to Travel with Your Dog Before You Die* attempts to capture the spectrum of rewarding travel experiences. While the book collects fifty great venues, it by no means attempts to rank the places discussed. Such ranking is, of course, largely subjective.

In the hope that you'll use this little book as a guide for embarking on adventures with your dog, we have provided brief "If You Go" information at the end of each location description, including dog-friendly lodging options and local pet supply stores. We've also included some guidelines for traveling internationally with your dog (pages 14–15), based on the best available information as we went to print. It's by no means a comprehensive list, but should give would-be travelers a starting point for planning their trip.

Most dog owners take joy in the everyday interactions their woofers provide—whether it be a belly scratch while enjoying that first cup of coffee in bed, or a visit to the local dog park. Yet a trip to a special destination that you can both enjoy can forge memories for a lifetime. It's our hope that this little book will inspire you to embark on new adventures together.

OPPOSITE:
Hiker and hound take in the Puget Sound near Seattle.

TRAVELING INTERNATIONALLY
WITH YOUR DOG

Traveling abroad with your dog will surely make for some lasting memories. But before you load up the car or book your flights, it's important to be clear on the vaccinations and paperwork your pup will need to cross international borders and enter a new country. On the following pages, we've provided useful websites for determining exactly what you'll need to take Fido abroad, based on the best available information at the time of this writing (September 2022).

A general note for all locations: Typically, you will need to have the required vaccinations and tests completed within a certain time frame before your arrival at your destination in order for them to be accepted. Double-check this information before you start the process. For travelers to European destinations, keep in mind that Europe uses fifteen-digit microchips, versus the ten-digit American standard. Medical records can be stored on these chips, so ensure that you chip your pet before getting any pre-travel vaccinations or tests. For extended travel in Europe, and to make border crossings easier, consider getting an EU Pet Passport. More information is available at aphis.usda.gov/aphis/pet-travel/by-country/eu/pet_travel-european_union_pet_passports.

The United States Department of Agriculture website (aphis.usda.gov) provides a useful overview of international travel with your pets, as do BringFido (bringfido.com) and Pet Travel (pettravel.com). The USDA website also includes the requirements that must be followed when you and your dog return to the United States after your time abroad. These can vary depending on which countries you visited, so be sure to give it a look before you book your travel.

AUSTRIA   For the most up-to-date requirements, consult the Austrian Federal Office for Consumer Health's rules: bavg.gv.at/en/import/living-animals/travel.

BELGIUM   Consult the Health, Food Chain Safety and Environment website of Belgium's Federal Public Service: www.health.belgium.be/en.

CANADA   Consult the Canadian Food Inspection Agency website: inspection.canada.ca/eng.

CZECH REPUBLIC The "Useful Links" page of the Consulate General for the Czech Republic's website keeps a list of entry requirements for traveling with pets: mzv.cz/consulate.newyork/en/useful_links.

FRANCE Consult the French customs website: www.douane.gouv.fr/demarche/vous-voyagez-avec-un-animal-de-compagnie-autre-que-carnivore-domestique-ou-oiseau-jusqua-5.

ITALY For the latest requirements, consult the Ministero della Salute: www.salute.gov.it.

JAPAN The procedures for bringing a pet dog into Japan are detailed on the website of the Ministry of Agriculture, Forestry and Fisheries: www.maff.go.jp. There may be a twelve-hour quarantine period imposed on incoming pets.

PORTUGAL Consult pettravel.com/immigration/Portugal.cfm.

SCOTLAND Entry requirements are laid out at www.gov.uk/bring-pet-to-great-britain. The UK has very stringent entry requirements for dogs, especially around rabies vaccinations. Check the website for the most up-to-date requirements before you book your travel.

SINGAPORE Consult the website of Singapore's Animal & Veterinary Service, a division of the National Park Service: www.nparks.gov.sg/avs. Note that there are some limitations pertaining to breeds, and a ten- or thirty-day pet quarantine period may be required upon arrival, depending on your country of origin. It's best to check this requirement before you book your travel.

SPAIN The most up to date requirements are on the website of the Ministerio de Agricultura, Pesca y Alimentación: www.mapa.gob.es/en.

SWITZERLAND The Swiss Federal Food Safety and Veterinary Office has a helpful tool to help you find your requirements at www.blv.admin.ch.

NEXT PAGE:
Many European cities, including Venice, welcome canine guests.

The Destinations

ANCHORAGE

RECOMMENDED BY **Mark Robokoff**

Dogs provide companionship for hundreds of millions of people around the world. For residents of the state of Alaska, the magnitude of dog/human integration approaches a new level, as Mark Robokoff explained: "Culturally in Alaska, there's an acceptance that if you're going to do something, you're more likely than not to bring your dog. There's no surprise; they are considered part of the family. Whether you're going four-wheeling, snow machining, fishing, or hunting, the dog is coming. Why is Alaska like this? It has to do with our official state sport—dog mushing. Every year during the Iditarod and Yukon Quest races, people go nuts. Most folks can tell you who is in the lead on any given day. The relationship between dog and man in mushing permeates the culture; the animal is not merely a sidekick, but assisting in what you're doing. The dog is part of the family—you're all in this together."

Anchorage, Alaska's largest city, holds over 40 percent of the forty-ninth state's population. And while it is by far the most urban outpost in the state's 665,400 square miles, it's still quite wild. The city—roughly the size of the state of Delaware and encircled by mountains and still intact glaciers—is home to some fifteen hundred moose, and is regularly visited by black and brown bears and Dall sheep; bald eagles are so plentiful that you may start to think of them like you do squirrels or pigeons! Ship Creek flows through the center of town, where Chinook and silver salmon return each summer to spawn. While many visitors use Anchorage as a staging area for cruises south through the Inside Passage or forays north to Denali National Park, Anchorage is also a great base to experience Alaska's wildlife and scenic beauty—either on foot on the city's 250 miles of trails, in nearby Chugach State Park (one of the largest in the nation), or with an outfitter that can spirit you a bit farther out of town for a "flightseeing" day trip.

OPPOSITE:
In Alaska, it's
customary for
dogs to join
their humans
on most outdoor
excursions.

It's believed that dogs have been used to pull sleds for at least eight thousand years. Though Alaska Natives have used dogs for eons to assist them in hunting and to offer protection from bears and other denizens of the tundra, it was the Klondike Gold Rush of 1896–1899 that brought the notion of dogs pulling sleds to the region, first to the Yukon and then to Alaska. Dogsleds provided an efficient way to carry supplies deep into the bush and to scout out potential new mining locations under wintry conditions. Dog mushing entered the national consciousness in 1925, when dogsled teams were used to deliver diphtheria antitoxin serum from Nenana to the village of Nome, which was racked with a debilitating outbreak of the disease. The seven-hundred-mile one-way trip was the inspiration for the Iditarod race, which now departs for Nome from the town of Willow and spans one thousand miles. Winners of the Iditarod have completed the race in just over eight days. ("Mushing," it should be noted, connotes the use of dogs to pull a load; all dogsledding is mushing, but not all mushing is dogsledding.)

When Mark opened his first retail operation in Anchorage after relocating from Minnesota, he saw it as a gift store for pets, stocked with items celebrating people's dogs—but his clientele was looking for *gear*. "People in Alaska don't just go for a walk," he said. "They do something more extreme—hiking, fishing, skiing. They wanted snow booties, bike-touring harnesses. One of our most popular products is a pair of ninety-dollar goggles for dogs that like to run behind their person's snow machine or ATV. [There are no snowmobiles in Alaska; only snow machines.] Hundred-fifty-dollar snow-suits are another popular item, as are CoyoteVests, chrome spike-covered vests that help protect chihuahuas and Yorkies from getting scooped up by an eagle or other predators."

So, what are some ways that Alaskans like to get outside with their dogs? "Beyond joining the family on hikes or fishing excursions, a lot of activities stem from dog mush-ing," Mark explained. "In the winter, there's skijoring, where the human is on skis and is pulled along by a dog or dogs. In the summer, there's bikejoring, where a dog or dogs pull a bike along; they're connected with an elastic line and wear a special harness. Another summer mushing variation is canicross, a fusion of cross-country running and mushing, where the dog runs in front wearing a canicross harness, connected to their human with a bungee line and canicross belt."

Will you see any of Alaska's iconic mammals when you're out walking the trails around Anchorage? Preferably not. "When you're out with your dog, you're trying *not* to encounter wildlife," Mark said. "You're going to see moose wherever you go, as there are few predators in town. You do your best not to see a bear, by wearing bear bells and making noise. If you're walking your dog off-leash, they need to respond quickly to recall. A dangerous situation can arise if you see a bear and your dog doesn't respond to your call; the dog will tend to run to the bear, the bear will react, the dog will run back to you . . . and the bear will follow."

When it comes time for dinner or an evening libation ("evening" is relative—in Anchorage, it's light for twenty-four hours in June and early July, and until almost midnight in August), most restaurants and the city's dozen breweries offer outdoor seating where dogs are permitted. If you decide to rent a car, Mark suggests a short drive down the Turnagain Arm to the town of Girdwood. "Girdwood has a strong dog culture, and the bars and restaurants there don't necessarily follow the 'no dogs inside' rule," he shared. The Seward Highway, the road to Girdwood, is designated an All-American Road by the Federal Highway Administration for its beauty and cultural value, and offers spectacular vistas of the Chugach and Kenai Mountains, plus a chance to spy Dall sheep and beluga whales.

MARK ROBOKOFF is the owner of AK Bark in Anchorage, Alaska. He rescues sight hounds and is on his sixth retired racing greyhound (Dutch). Mark enjoys hiking Alaska's backcountry and placing improbably balanced rock stacks in remote places for others to discover. He is also very active in local theater and film productions; his acting credits can be found on IMDb or at MarkRobokoff.com.

If You Go

▶ **Getting There:** Anchorage is served by many carriers, including Alaska Airlines (800-252-7522; alaskaair.com).

▶ **Best Time to Visit:** Most prefer to visit Anchorage during the summer months, though winter has its appeal for some.

▶ **Accommodations:** More than twenty hotels in Anchorage welcome dogs. See the full list at Visit Anchorage (907-276-4118; anchorage.net).

▶ **Supplies:** AK Bark Gifts (907-349-1700; akbarkgifts.com) has the gear you need to get outside with your dog in the forty-ninth state.

JASPER

RECOMMENDED BY **Matt Campbell**

"Before I even got my dog, I was doing a lot of camping," Matt Campbell began. "That was part of my decision to get a dog, actually. We wanted to bring Ellie, our shepard rescue, with us when we went into the mountains."

Nature lovers who set their sights on the rugged Canadian Rockies tend to beeline straight for Banff, Canada's most popular national park. However, those who have the appetite to travel two hundred miles farther north along the same scenic mountain range will be greeted with Jasper National Park—a protected evergreen paradise that is almost double in square mileage and half as populated as its southern sister. "The drive into the valley is picturesque," reflected Matt. "It's less developed, less commercial, and you see fewer tourists. Both parks have high-end luxury hotels and things like that. But Jasper has a certain amount of ruggedness that other parks don't have."

Summer is the cherished hiking season, when fields of high-altitude wildflowers are in bloom, and dips in azure mountain lakes keep the balmy heat at bay. Dogs are welcome in Jasper National Park, with regulations typically requiring that they be on-leash and under voice control, so the norm is that your dog will hit the trail by your side (with a few exceptions—some trails are signed as protected thoroughfares for caribou migration). "We love hiking with Ellie," continued Matt. "Sulphur Skyline is probably my favorite trail. You start at the hot springs in the town of Jasper, and go all the way up to the peak of the mountain. There are switchbacks and scrambling, so be prepared—it's not easy. But if you have the ability, it's a wonderful experience. Being outside, breathing the fresh mountain air, moving your body, and right there is your dog, running alongside you, soaking it up, loving the smells . . . it's a tremendous feeling. And then before you know it, you're at the top of mountain. It feels incredibly

OPPOSITE:
Jasper National
Park has miles
of majestic
dog-friendly trails
and lakes.

special, a real gift. These are the kinds of places that not everyone gets to see, especially not with their dog."

It's hard to find a hike with a bad view in Jasper. The only limiting factor is the energy level you and your dog bring to the table. Some favorites include the Valley of the Five Lakes trail, a moderately difficult three-mile route that's perfect for introducing dogs to hiking. For elevation junkies, the six miles of Wilcox Pass farther down the Icefields Parkway will test your endurance. The six bridges of Maligne Canyon, the deepest canyon in the Canadian Rockies, is another favorite area, a wonderland of bridges and waterfalls with a variety of moderate trails to pick from. Consider leaving early to avoid the crowds, and pack a towel in the car for your pup's post-hike muddy paws. If you visit in the winter, a guided ice walk takes you on an exploration of the canyon's crystalline floor, including walking under frozen waterfall cascades.

"Jasper really is an all-season destination," said Matt. "You can hike and canoe in the spring and summer, but in the winter you can ski, rent snowshoes, and enjoy acres of fresh powder. We came with Ellie one year, with an extra-long leash and a coat, and did an incredible snow hike around Maligne Lake. Ellie was frolicking through it all. She was pretty tired at the end of the day, but she loved it. You can also drive up to the Miette Hot Springs and soak off the cold. And then there are the Columbia Icefields, far from town, which are worth a visit." It's worth noting that, unfortunately, for safety reasons dogs are not allowed on the glacier tour, but this is roughly the only area where that is the case.

Jasper National Park covers nearly 6,835 square miles of wilderness, and most amenities are contained in the charming little village of Jasper itself, located in the center of the park. "Jasper is big enough to have everything you would need in a resort town, but it's small enough that you can walk across it," reflected Matt. "There's plenty of great, dog-friendly restaurants. Jasper Brewing Company is a favorite of ours. There's a fantastic pizza and steak house called L&W that we've also enjoyed. If you want to drive, just a little bit outside the park there is a brewery called Folding Mountain, which we always like to visit while we're there."

Lodging options range from glamorous to rustic. For a plushier stay away from the "bustle" of downtown Jasper, drive a few minutes north along Yellowhead Highway to the wood-and-stone-paneled Pyramid Lake Resort. The hotel welcomes pets, has epic lakeviews, and hosts a few trailheads. Farther north is the Miette Mountain Cabins resort, which features a cluster of alpine cottages, an on-site restaurant, and a few shops to cover essentials. If you prefer to stay in the centrality of Jasper's town, a number of dog-friendly options are available.

Of course, camping is open year-round. "The last time I went, Whistler's campground had just gone through a multimillion-dollar revamp, and they are super dog-friendly. They have an amphitheater and a playground for kids. We also have something here in Canada called oTENTiks. They're part canvas tent, part log cabin. You can rent them in advance and have one waiting when you arrive. If you don't have your own RV or tent but still want to camp, it's a wonderful option. They even provide you with firewood.

"Ultimately, Jasper might be more friendly than other places in the Canadian Rockies," Matt concluded. "Possibly because it gets a little less busy. If your dog is a little skittish about people and traffic, it could be better than some of the other, more crowded park options. I think dogs really help us stay present in the moment, allow us to experience things as if we were there for the first time. And Jasper is a wonderful place to be present."

MATT CAMPBELL is the pet-parent of Dogtor Ellie Sattler, a shepherd rescue who shares her antics on Instagram at @dogtor_ellie_sattler. Matt and Ellie live and work in Edmonton, Alberta. When not camping, they can be found on Twitter refusing to commit to one brand. Matt often tweets about Ellie, *Star Trek*, movies, and how Edmonton's public transit will never be sufficient until they end car-centric thinking.

If You Go

▶ **Getting There:** Jasper's regional airport is served by Jasper by Air (888-276-6660; flyjasper.ca). Flights are limited and typically only run between Calgary and Vancouver. Another option is to fly into Calgary or Edmonton (both international airports) and either rent a car or reserve a bus ticket to take you to Jasper's doorstep.
▶ **Best Time to Visit:** Summer hiking usually begins mid-June and ends in September. Winter sports tend to be open mid-November to mid-May.
▶ **Accommodations:** Tourism Jasper lists a variety of reliable options at www.jasper.travel.
▶ **Supplies:** The Jasper Pet Outpost (825-422-0010; jasperpetoutpost.ca) has food, toys, kenneling, day care, and self-serve dog-washing stations.

Arizona

BISBEE

RECOMMENDED BY **Amy Burkert**

"My husband and I first came to Bisbee in 2011," said Amy Burkert. "We had heard about this cool little town, and we were coming across I-10 and decided we would swing down and check it out. Initially I didn't care for it. But you have to understand that Bisbee has one main street. So we hung out on that main street and never veered off. A few years later, we came a second time when my parents were in town, since it was on the way to Tombstone. And again, I thought, 'This isn't really for me.' Finally, we came a third time. We were in Tucson in the winter and just wanted to get away for a weekend. But that time, I came across a trail that utilizes the staircases—Bisbee is an old mining town, built into a canyon, and a network of staircases connect the streets that go up the canyon walls— and climbing the staircases, that's when I really saw Bisbee for the first time. It was the staircases themselves, and they led me to the people. I was enthralled."

Sitting over five thousand feet above sea level in southern Arizona's Mule Mountains, Bisbee is a town you might miss if you were zooming by on the freeway. However, to those in the know, the former copper-mining village is a haven of art, music, eclectic architecture, above-average friendly residents, and a supremely dog-friendly culture. "As we were walking around and our rescue Myles was wagging his tail at everybody, everybody wanted to say hello to him," Amy recalled. "We started talking to people out on their lawns; people were clearly used to chatting with each other like friendly neighbors. On one staircase, we had to stop and catch our breath, and we're looking out over one particularly nice Victorian house. And then the owner came around the corner and just offered to show us his place. That's just how nice the people are here. After that visit, we came back to spend the following winter here. And then we decided never to leave."

When Bisbee's mine shut down in the early 1970s, housing values crashed. The town was in a bust. Some people traded their homes for cars so they could simply get out. "But then a bunch of hippies moved in," continued Amy, "and completely transformed it. It's a really unusual, funky little town. There's tons of art galleries, live music is everywhere, and so many displays of public art. Because we're in a canyon, there's lots of retaining walls, and the artists paint murals on them, embed them with charms and colored glass. And it's intensely walkable—everything you need is within walking distance. You park your car and can walk just about everywhere."

In addition to its thriving arts scene, the town's architecture is worth admiring at a walking pace. Vintage miners' shacks, colorful hippie cottages, and lovingly preserved Old West Victorians all climb the hillsides above the valley. "The city itself is a national historical landmark," noted Amy, "so the little old houses are not being torn down and replaced with McMansions; they are being maintained.

"We spent twelve years in an RV, going across America to map out pet-friendly locations, and so much of what we saw is that our country is turning into box stores and strip malls," she continued. "You could fall asleep in Connecticut and wake up in Kansas and not entirely know it unless you asked. But the character here in Bisbee is what really drew us in. There aren't a lot of places like this anymore."

Bisbee's downtown is effectively one street: Tombstone Canyon Road. The bars, shops, and cafés on the main drag are almost universally pet-friendly, especially Bisbee Coffee Company and High Desert Market and Café, which boast particularly spacious and welcoming patios. But the real magic of Bisbee begins once you get off the main road. "There's really no going wrong," said Amy. Off the main street, some notables include Kafka coffee shop and Old Bisbee Brewing Company, both of which allow dogs inside or in the courtyard, and St. Elmo Bar, which holds the record as the longest continually running bar in Arizona (it opened in 1902), and where dogs are welcome to join you on an adjacent barstool.

The magic of Bisbee is in the walking, and the best routes involve the famous staircases that climb the canyon walls. For a quick walk, go to the end of OK Street and take the established trail up the hill, which ends at a decorated altar and cluster of white crosses. For a longer hike, pick up the Ridge Trail from Adams Avenue for a spectacular route overlooking the Chiricahua Mountains. "Another fun day trip is to actually go over to Mexico," reflected Amy. "We're only about twenty minutes from a little town off the side of the border called Naco. It makes for a fun Taco Tuesday: tacos in Naco." Another side trip is to head to Kartchner Caverns State Park. Dogs can't go into the caverns, but the trails around them are supremely beautiful and very dog-friendly.

"The reason I find traveling with pets so important is that when we just follow our routine day to day back home, when we look back over our pet's lifetime, we realize all our time spent with them blurs together," Amy concluded. "But when you travel with your pet, you remember specific moments: The day you went hiking in Colorado for the first time; the day you took them to the beach for the first time. Those moments stand out. And those are the moments we hold on to after our pets are gone. The bond you build while traveling is so wonderful."

AMY BURKERT launched GoPetFriendly, a website that inspires people to do more with their pets and provides the resources they need to make that happen, in 2009. With more than sixty-five thousand pet-friendly listings across the US and Canada, GoPetFriendly makes it easy to find pet-friendly places to stay and things to do. After launching GoPetFriendly, Amy and her husband, Rod, traveled full-time in their Winnebago with their dogs for more than twelve years. With two hundred thousand miles behind her, Amy shares pet-friendly destination advice and practical pet-travel tips on the GoPetFriendly blog. She also self-published the award-winning book *The Ultimate Pet Friendly Road Trip*, which highlights the number one pet-friendly attraction in each of the lower forty-eight states.

If You Go

▶ **Getting There:** Bisbee is a little under two hours' drive from Tucson, whose airport is served by several carriers, with many direct routes on Southwest (800-435-9792; southwest.com).

▶ **Best Time to Visit:** Many people's favorite time to visit is July and August. This is monsoon season, when the mountain grasses and flowers bloom, and the afternoon clouds block the worst of the summer heat.

▶ **Accommodations:** Many of Bisbee's hotels are pet-friendly, including the Copper Queen Hotel (520-432-2216; copperqueen.com) and the Jonquil Motel (520-432-7371; thejonquil.com).

▶ **Supplies:** Bisbee is a small town. Although there is an animal shelter and a few veterinarians, most visitors purchase pet food and basic gear at the local grocery store.

TUCSON

RECOMMENDED BY **Irene McHugh**

Tucson embodies the iconic Old West like few other cities can. Saguaro cactuses grow proudly across front yards, and the Santa Catalina Mountains paint the horizon in vibrant reds and oranges. Nature lovers scale peaks for sweeping views of the city and surrounding desert, and astronomy buffs take advantage of the famously clear skies. Cowboy life is alive and well at the annual Cochise Cowboy Poetry & Music Gathering in nearby Sierra Vista, or year-round at the Arizona Folklore Preserve.

All good cowboy ranches have a dog or two on hand to assist with the daily chores and keep the other animals secure. Even though Tucson has modernized past its pioneer days, the city honors the legacy between man and dog by being one of the most canine-friendly places in the country.

"I actually didn't have dogs until I moved to Tucson," Irene McHugh began. "Tucson is a different kind of city. It doesn't have strong boundaries. There's a very seamless feel between Tucson and the rest of Pima County. It has a smaller, calmer, unbroken, residential feel, and the presence of many parks makes it a great place to take or train a dog."

Some favorite parks for pooches include Brandi Fenton Memorial Park, a fifty-seven-acre oasis of greenery and splash pads in the northwest of the city. "It's huge," said Irene. "Within the park there are basketball courts, a little soccer athletic club, a water park for kids, a butterfly garden, and three dedicated areas for small, medium, and large dogs. There are loads of kids and dogs running around, but there's also lots of space. If you're training your dog to be socialized, this is a perfect place."

Just south of Brandi Fenton is the local favorite OK Feed & Pet Supply, a mom-and-pop pet supplier with a reputation for impressive, unique treats. Tucson's most popular dog walk, a paved, multiuse trail that runs through 136 miles of Pima County, is simply

OPPOSITE:
A pair of
goldendoodles
hike through
Saguaro cacti
in Arizona.

referred to as "The Loop." Visitors can almost think of it as a highway, with entrances and exits taking walkers to some of the county's most charming and bustling enclaves. "Right off the Loop is St. Philip's Plaza, closer to the Catalina Foothills part of town," Irene said. "They have restaurants with lots of pet-friendly patios. On the weekend they have a little outdoor farmers' market. It's a great place to have breakfast, take in some sights, and enjoy the day with your dog.

"You have to be a little creative where you take your dog in the summer," noted Irene. "I always get up early to beat the heat, and you'll usually have parks almost to yourself at that time. But keep in mind, Tucson is also built for heat. It's a good idea to have booties for hot asphalt and carry a water bowl with you, but there's also lots of misters on patios, and water stops in parks and on the Loop."

Early risers should consider driving north for a visit to Catalina State Park, which marks the base of the majestic Santa Catalina mountain range; a bounty of desert flora, craggy peaks, and waterfalls. "There are tons of dog-friendly trails," said Irene. "Do the Canyon Loop trail; I think I must have done that one once a week. Dogs have to be leashed, as there are many wild animals around, and the rare rattlesnake might try to say hello. But it's a spectacular experience."

Back in town, another favorite destination is La Encantada, a spacious upscale shopping district that pampers pups and humans alike. "They have tons of restaurants, shopping, and an AJ's Fine Foods grocery store," Irene noted. "The merchants have water bowls outside their shops and are very welcoming. I took one of our Labradoodles, Bernie, to a shop up there once, and the owner came outside, looked at the water bowl, and said 'Oh, I need to top that off!' And she actually started pouring bottled water into the bowl. Misters are also prevalent, so this is one area you won't need to put booties on your dog's feet."

Other cool options include the Tucson Botanical Gardens, where you can buy a summer membership for yourself, and also for your four-legged friend. "It pays for itself quite quickly," mused Irene. "There is so much shade from the plants and trees. You can walk at your own pace, and there are lots of benches to rest. If, for whatever reason, you or your dog want to get out of the sun but you still want to get outside, this is the perfect place."

"A favorite memory I have of Tucson," Irene concluded, "is of these pack walks we used to do with the Complete Canine, a therapy dog training school. When we went to the University of Arizona, there would be college students actually waiting to meet the dogs when we went through every Thursday. These college kids missed their home dogs so much, so we'd always stop and the dogs would get all their love and pets.

"On one of these trips, I had Lizzie on-leash and we came around the corner, and the students were in a new spot, not where they normally are. But Lizzie went down into a play bow, and she recognized them anyway, right away. So I started walking over to the new spot, and I said, 'Hey, somebody recognizes you, would you like to say hi?' One of the girls got up, and she was so earnest, and said, 'This is the highest honor, to be recognized by this dog!' and they met like old friends. That's very Tucson."

IRENE MCHUGH is cofounder of the award-winning therapy dog blog *McSquare Doodles* (mcsquaredoodles.com) and dog mom for the McSquare pack. After retiring from teaching middle school students, she transitioned to using those same skills to train her two Australian Labradoodles. She's a founding member of the All Pet Collaborative, a member of the Dog Writers Association of America, and a supporting member of the International Association of Animal Behavior Consultants. Irene believes in helping all pet parents find time to train their dogs so they can build stronger relationships. The resources at *McSquare Doodles* help pet parents feel less overwhelmed around training and working toward therapy dog certification.

If You Go

▶ **Getting There:** Tucson International Airport is served by several carriers, with many direct routes on Southwest (800-435-9792; southwest.com).

▶ **Best Time to Visit:** Summer can see temperatures of over 100°F and monsoon rains. Late spring and early autumn offer more temperate weather. Winters are mild and sunny, offering a wonderful time to be outside and the height of the tourist season.

▶ **Accommodations:** Visit Tucson has a list of hotels at visittucson.org.

▶ **Supplies:** Tucson has many pet stores, but OK Feed & Pet Supply (520-325-0122; okfeedaz.com) is a local favorite.

MARGARET RIVER

RECOMMENDED BY **Tommi Nordström**

"Many people don't realize just how large Australia is," Tommi Nordström ventured. "And they often know little about the state of Western Australia, which makes up one-third of the country. Western Australia has massive outback areas, and in the north, places that are home to Indigenous people. Further south, below the city of Perth, is the Margaret River region. The mild climate is well-suited to growing grapes and has become one of Australia's best-known wine regions. Margaret River is also blessed with many soft-sand beaches and big swells that have made it a famous surfing spot. There's a nice blend of small towns and open countryside there. The mix of beaches, forest-and wineries make Margaret River a wonderful place to visit. And dogs are very welcome."

Western Australia comprises nearly one million square miles, shared among fewer than three million inhabitants . . . with a great majority of those people in and around the capital city of Perth. The town of Margaret River sits 170 miles to the south, near the point where its eponymous river approaches the Indian Ocean (a sandbar often blocks the fresh water from actually meeting the sea). The area was home to the Wadandi people for more than fifty thousand years. European settlers arrived in the region in the 1830s, and Margaret River initially developed as a timber-harvesting region. It was in the mid-1960s, after a research paper by a University of Western Australia agronomist named John Gladstones, that the region's potential as a viticultural area was recognized. Soon after, the area's first vineyards were established, and not long after that, surfers discovered some noteworthy breaks west of town—including Main Break, the Box, and Joey's Nose—drawing still more visitors to the region. Many of the woodlands and beaches allow dogs. "Dogs aren't allowed in national parks in Australia," Tommi noted. "But there's not many national parks in the Margaret River area. So dogs have great access."

OPPOSITE:
Many dogs enjoy
the beach, and
in Australia,
more and more
beaches—like
this sandy stretch
near Margaret
River—are open
to canines.

The general acceptance of dogs in day-to-day Australian life is definitely increasing. "It used to be that you had working dogs, or pet dogs that stayed at home," Tommi explained. "But now dogs are accompanying their people more frequently. At the pub, visiting friends, even at some offices, dogs are welcome. They are more and more part of your everyday social life. And the number of dogs is increasing; almost fifty percent of households have dogs. This being said, dogs are still not allowed on public transportation, and they can't go inside of restaurants. We have some catching up to do. But as people's attitudes are changing, our legislation and the rules of hospitality venues have to evolve."

Many visitors to the Margaret River region come for a chance to sample its fine wines. In the fifty years since its first vineyards were established, the area's soil and climate have proven favorable for both white and red varietals, including cabernet sauvignon, merlot, shiraz, chardonnay, sauvignon blanc, chenin blanc, and sémillon. "Many of the wineries have realized that if you travel from the city to visit, you're likely to take your dog with you," Tommi explained. "If you're not dog-friendly, you're missing out on business. Though dogs are allowed inside in some cellar doors [inside wineries], most have outdoor seating where dogs are welcome." A few of Tommi's favorite Margaret River wineries to visit include Woody Nook and Happs Wines. "Woody Nook is not just a winery, but also has a dog-friendly restaurant adjoining," he described. "The proprietors are very welcoming to dogs. Happs has a cellar door that doesn't permit dogs, but they also have a large lawn area. At any point, there are hundreds of people outside having picnics with their dogs and enjoying a glass of wine. Gourmet picnic baskets and wine are sold on premises."

Visitors will find a broad range of lodging options around Margaret River. "It's relatively affordable," Tommi noted, "especially compared to some of the other wine-growing regions like Yarra Valley and Hunter Valley. You can find cabins and dog-friendly campsites in a rural, wooded setting or waterfront, beach-style accommodations."

Australia is known for many things—kangaroos, the Sydney Opera House, and Crocodile Dundee among them. But perhaps it is most celebrated for its beaches. The land down under has more than ten thousand of them, and more and more are open to humankind's best friend. "As in other areas of dog inclusion, Australia is improving," Tommi reflected. "As of now, there are six hundred dog-friendly beaches here. Some are twenty-four hours off-leash; others require dogs to be on-leash during busy hours but can be off the lead in the morning before nine A.M. or ten A.M. and in the late afternoon after four P.M. or five P.M.

"The best part of travel with our dog is the beach. Our Groodle, Lumi, loves the sand and the water; he doesn't even need a ball to have fun. He's picked up bodysurfing a bit, and that seems to be the ultimate fun for him. Though around Margaret River, the waves and currents can be strong, and dogs [and their people] need to be aware of it." When asked if surfers ever take their dogs along on their boards, Tommi paused before answering: "When the surf isn't too high, I've seen people take their dogs along. But I wouldn't recommend it unless you're a good surfer and your dog is an exceptional swimmer." Do great white sharks pose a risk to human and canine swimmers? "There's no question that great whites are around," Tommi said. "Though media reports may make it sound like a shark eats someone every day, attacks are extremely rare."

According to the Florida Museum of Natural History's International Shark Attack File (which documents all known shark attacks since 1958), the odds of being killed by a shark are 1 in 3,748,067 . . . which means you're more likely to die from encountering an asteroid.

TOMMI NORDSTRÖM cofounded Pupsy (pupsy.com.au) in 2017. It's Australia's largest online platform for dog owners to find and book dog-friendly places and services. It's a bit like Tripadvisor, just a little furrier. Before Pupsy, he served in senior marketing roles at Beach Life Australia and British American Tobacco. Based near Sydney, Tommi loves adventuring around his adopted country with his Groodle, Lumi.

If You Go

▶ **Getting There:** Many will fly to Perth, which is served by a number of carriers, including Qantas (800-227-4500; qantas.com). The Busselton Margaret River Airport is served from Melbourne on Jetstar (866-397-8170; jetstar.com).

▶ **Best Time to Visit:** Margaret River enjoys a mild climate year-round; the coolest and wettest months of the year fall in the Austral winter (June–August).

▶ **Accommodations:** Pupsy (pupsy.com.au) lists a range of dog-friendly lodging options in and around Margaret River.

▶ **Supplies:** Margaret River offers a number of pet purveyors, including Margaret River Produce and Pet (+61 08 9757 2447; mrproduce.com.au).

VIENNA

RECOMMENDED BY **Amanda Klecker**

"Initially I was worried about traveling to Vienna, because it was so cold, and I thought we'd only be able to go onto patios," Amanda Klecker began. "I assumed finding places to take our dog would be this huge challenge. But then I quickly realized it wasn't an issue at all. We could bring Jonathan, our Chihuahua mix, inside literally everywhere we went."

Austria's elegant capital is known for its gilded baroque architecture, manicured parks, and posh cafés. Hand in hand with a love of refined things, it seems, comes a love of canines. "The Viennese are just used to having dogs around; they are part of the culture," reflected Amanda. "Something that's really signature to Vienna are these opulent cafés that feature ornately decorated desserts. These places are so upscale—everything is gold leaf, crown molding upon crown molding, crystal chandeliers. And you can walk into one of these places for brunch or lunch, and the staff greets you with a smile and a 'of course you can have a chair for your dog.' So again, it's not just that you can bring your dog. It's that your dog is *invited*."

Although well-behaved pets are both common and welcome indoor guests at the vast majority of Vienna's famous cafés, be sure to check out Café Landtmann in particular. This plush, wood-paneled nineteenth-century coffeehouse is famous for its artful espressos and has been frequented by Sigmund Freud and Paul McCartney. On your way, stop by the nearby Rathauspark and take in the majestic neo-Gothic facade of Vienna's city hall. If you visit during Christmas, be sure not to miss the incredible light displays and traditional Christmas markets that decorate the park. Across town, other notable eateries include Café Prückel, on the corner of the manicured Stadtpark, with its bunches of springtime tulips and parade of marble statues. "Prückel is an iconic, 1950s-style coffeehouse, but with waiters in tuxedos and dog art on the walls. Keep in mind, Landtmann

OPPOSITE: Vienna's elegant cafés serve decadent coffees, grand pastries, and luxurious cakes to humans— and dogs are welcome guests.

and Prückel aren't 'dog cafés' as we're used to thinking about them. They are iconic coffeehouses, and people go there to eat lunch, have a drink, et cetera. It's just that sometimes, their dog is right next to them." Wherever you visit, try the *topfenknödel*, a quintessentially Austrian dish of quark-and-flour dumplings, sometimes stuffed with jam or chocolate sauce, or a slice of Esterházy torte, a sponge cake that blends cinnamon, cocoa, almond, vanilla, hazelnuts, rum, and buttercream into an elegant six-layered tower.

Vienna has no shortage of immaculately kept public parks where you can stroll with your dog; just be sure to mind the signs for the rare *hundeverbot* ("dogs not allowed") areas, and know that while dogs are common, leashes are the norm. On public transit, dogs are welcome to join their owners—Vienna is one of the few cities in the world where this is permitted—but muzzles are often required, and the rule enforced, so be sure to have one on hand before heading out for the day. Throughout the city, keep an eye out for *hundezones*, designated off-leash areas where dogs can run free. There are at least three in every district, most within the public parks.

A great place to visit is the Prater, an amusement park with roller coasters, games, and the oldest Ferris wheel in the world. "Dogs can't go on the rides, and you probably wouldn't want to take them anyway," Amanda said. "But you can enjoy the fair and the games with your dog along for the fun.

"When we first went to Vienna, it was for New Year's 2020. The government blocks out the whole downtown area of the city, so no cars can come through. And it's just this big party in the streets, rows of pop-up shops, concert stages, DJs, Christmas markets, food, drink, everyone is dancing . . . I heard it was one of the biggest New Year's Eve celebrations in the world, and I believe it. We took Jonathan to the parts we thought he would like, not too crowded or congested. He was definitely not the only dog. We were eating and having cocktails, and he was right with us. Nobody batted an eye."

When it's time to find a place to rest for the night, visitors have their pick of hotels. But discerning tourists might do well to consider a stay at Hotel Sacher, a plush, wood-paneled nineteenth-century hotel that has hosted the likes of Queen Elizabeth II and John F. Kennedy. Anna Sacher, the hotel's famous, cigar-smoking founder who took over the hotel from her late husband at age twenty-three and turned it into a cultural institution, was said to be inseparable from her French bulldogs. A respectful fondness for canine guests has been integral to the hotel's culture ever since. Guest rooms decorated with chandeliers and damask duvets also come prepared with doggy blankets, towels, feeding bowls, and, of course, special beds for each dog. Pet-sitters are available upon request—which may come in handy in the event that you're in town for Vienna's famous springtime ball season or if you're attending one of the city's famous operas.

"Normally, when you go on vacation with your dog, you aim to find places where they can join you," Amanda said, "but ultimately you know there are certain restrictions on what experiences they can participate in. In Vienna, we didn't have to find compromises. I felt like we actually had an authentic experience with that city."

AMANDA KLECKER is the proud dog mom of Jonathan Warren, a Chihuahua mix and former death row inmate at a high-kill shelter in Georgia. He was saved by a rescue wagon that brought him to Connecticut, where he was adopted by his new family. He now lives a life of love and luxury on Manhattan's Upper East Side. Jonathan Warren has traveled across the world and throughout the United States showcasing dog-friendly adventures that include one-of-a-kind experiences such as an exclusive tour of Veuve Clicquot in Reims and chartering an antique saloon boat through the Amsterdam canals. From Barcelona to Brooklyn and all the places in between, he uses his platform to increase awareness for pet adoption and raise money for animal rescue organizations.

If You Go

▶ **Getting There:** Vienna International Airport is served by several airlines, but is the hub for Austrian Airlines (800-843-0002; austrian.com).

▶ **Best Time to Visit:** Christmas markets and city light displays make winter a particularly colorful time to visit. Spring plays host to the famous ball season, and summer has the least rain and warmest temperatures.

▶ **Accommodations:** Hotel Sacher asks that you mention your pet at the time of booking (+43 1 514560; sacher.com).

▶ **Supplies:** Vienna has several pet shops. Consider a stop into Dogstyler (+43 02921 944 7620 0; dogstyler.at), an upscale dog boutique and bakery, for all your last-minute fashion needs.

6

DESTINATION

BRUGES

RECOMMENDED BY **Susie Senecal**

"In Bruges, a NO DOGS ALLOWED sign is the exception, not the rule," Susie Senecal began. "It's shocking when you come upon a place that isn't welcoming to dogs. London was not quite that way when my husband and I left in 2016. I recall being asked to leave the garden area of a pub for having a dog, though we were surrounded by smokers. I remember one of the first times we visited a pub in Bruges. It was November, cold and dark, and my husband, Nick, stuck his head through the door to see if it was okay to come in with our dog. It was. We chose the table that was nearest the door so we wouldn't be in the middle of activity with our dog, who went under the table. The landlord came over and said, 'None of that!' He put our dog on a chair and offered her a snack from a cookie jar. She was served before us! It makes sense: Dogs are an important part of our lives, and they enjoy being with people. They can be an essential part of your life in Bruges."

Bruges sits near the northwest corner of Belgium in the province of West Flanders, not far from the North Sea. It was this proximity to the sea that made Bruges a major trading center in medieval times, a crucial link between northern Europe and the Mediterranean. Bruges was a hub of the wool and spice trades in the fourteenth and fifteenth centuries, and during this golden age pioneered the use of many financial instruments, including promissory notes and the world's first stock exchange. The city's great wealth yielded dramatic architecture (with many neighborhoods connected by canals) and fostered the arts, including the origins of the Flemish school of oil painting. Unfortunately, the flow of commerce slowed to a trickle when the channel connecting Bruges to the sea began to silt up in the early sixteenth century, and the city was soon relegated to a less significant role on the world stage. A few centuries later, however, the fruits of Bruges's earlier affluence would attract worldly attention again, as tourists began

OPPOSITE:
Bruges is dotted with many canals, crossed by bridges dating back to medieval times.

to visit to take in its striking medieval architecture. Today, the historic center of Bruges (the Old Town district) is recognized as a UNESCO World Heritage site, and is considered one of Europe's best-preserved medieval cities.

One of the great joys of Bruges is to be had simply by walking about. "Stepping out into the Old Town is like walking into a fairy tale," Susie said. "When we first began visiting, we thought we'd need to go on a guided tour. But it's not like that. You needn't search out the sights—they are right there within a few minutes' walk of each other. To me, it's a lovely atmosphere, whatever time of year. In the winter, I find it almost Dickensian—dark and smoky. In the summer when there's a bright blue sky, the pretty views are doubled by the reflection from the canals." On your walks around the city—and for that matter, at many of the attractions—your dog is most welcome. "The museums, food markets and most of the churches don't allow dogs," Susie explained, "but stores and cafés welcome them. If you go into a café or chocolate shop, the proprietor will offer your dog water. We love to walk our dog along the canals, crossing back and forth over the humpbacked stone bridges. Eventually, you'll find yourself in the Markt [Market Square]. It's a great place to sit and do some people- and dog-watching. If it's raining, you can head into one of the bars, coffee or tea shops looking onto the Markt. Wherever you are in Bruges, there's always somewhere to stop off for some refreshment."

The Markt is also the site of the city's most famous landmark, the Belfry of Bruges. It dates back to the thirteenth century, stands over 272 feet tall, and is home to forty-seven carillon bells; 366 steps will take you to the top for stunning views of the city and surrounding lowlands. (The belfry, as some moviegoers may recall, figures in a pivotal scene in the Martin McDonagh black comedy *In Bruges*.)

You can easily walk your feet off in Bruges, gazing up at the spires and other architectural embellishments. But it's also fun to take in the city from a boat or carriage. "There are five boat companies that lead tours on the canals," Susie explained. "They all do the same course. The captains are real characters—they tell their own story of the city as they point out the sites; it's not a canned speech like some tour companies. You get a different view than from the cobbled streets. Dogs are welcome, of course. They're also welcome on the horse-drawn carriages that depart from the Markt. Again, the horsemen are all locals, and you get their personal perspective of the city."

While museums are generally off-limits for dogs, one welcomes canines—and it happens to be a museum of beer! "The [Bruges] Beer Experience is a favorite stop for us,"

Susie enthused. "The bottom floors tell the story of Belgian beer, and at the top there's a bar. We once had guests who didn't have dogs with them, and they borrowed ours to take them out for a walk. Our dogs took them straight to the beer museum." Whether you visit a waffle stand near the Markt or one of Bruges's Michelin-starred restaurants, you'll find the food excellent. "Our food and beer are superb," Susie added. "During the COVID lockdowns, only essential shops were open. Both chocolate shops and beer stores remained in business." That says something about priorities in Bruges.

If you're lucky enough to secure a room at the Doghouse, a dog-embracing B&B in the heart of the old city, your pooch might enjoy a beer, too. Susie offers her dog guests Snuffle, an alcohol-free chicken- or beef-flavored "beer" for dogs. (There's also a lounge on the premises where their owners can slake their thirst.)

SUSIE SENECAL came to Bruges with her husband, Nick, after a successful career in London's fashion industry. Initially, it was a weekend escape; now it's home. Today they operate the Doghouse, a renovated eighteenth-century townhouse-cum-B&B in Bruges's old city.

If You Go

▶ **Getting There:** Most international travelers will fly into Brussels, which is served by many carriers. It's an hour train ride from Brussels to Bruges on Belgian National Railways (belgianrail.be/en).

▶ **Best Time to Visit:** You'll find the mildest temperatures in Bruges in the summertime, though summer comes with larger crowds. But as Susie pointed out, there are pleasures in Bruges throughout the year.

▶ **Accommodations:** Many properties in Bruges cater to dogs, including the Doghouse (+32 468 311 511; thedoghousebruges.co.uk), which offers dog-friendly bikes to visitors (as well as dog beer). A full list of dog-friendly properties resides at Visit Bruges (visitbruges .be/en).

▶ **Supplies:** Cat & Dog Shop (+32 050 33 01 02; catanddogshop.be) is near city center and has your dog's needs covered.

REVELSTOKE

RECOMMENDED BY **Niki Perry**

"Revelstoke has to be one of the most beautiful places on earth," Niki Perry began. "It's a hippie town for sure, very laid-back, lots of organic food and people living very holistic lifestyles. The town is nestled in a mountain valley, and nature is something we don't take for granted. What there isn't is a lot of people. The trails aren't full. The wilderness is the wilderness. And dogs are just about everywhere."

Revelstoke has long seasons, with hot green summers and snowy winters. The powder on the mountains tends to start accumulating in November and clings all the way through May. "Winter sports are huge here," Niki explained. "Skiing, snowshoeing, snowmobiling, sledding, everything. And the dogs love to play in the snow with you." Snowshoeing is a particular favorite human and canine pastime, especially at the Seven Bridges Trail, which begins at the Mount Macpherson recreation area and meanders through 2.5 miles of winter wonderland. More adventurous winter sportsmen can opt to hit ski trails with their pups. At the Revelstoke Nordic Ski Club, the Roadway Ramble, Easy Al's, BCIT, Short Hop, and Ellie's are all routes that welcome dogs. "There are also many little parks along the Columbia River—we just call them 'the flats,'" Niki continued. "The community comes together down there. You can go down there, build a fire, the dogs play in the snow, you can take the kids on the snowmobile. It's really fun.

"Because we're at the valley bottom of some really beautiful mountains and we get tons of snow, funny things can happen," said Niki. "Sometimes, the snow gets so high, dogs can just walk over the fence of their backyard. But because it's a small community, a friend or neighbor will always give you a call on the phone and tell you, 'Oh hi, I just saw your dog walking by, just so you know!' I once caught my dog wandering over the snow-covered backyards to play with his best friend Boxer, who lived just down the road."

OPPOSITE:
The mountain town of Revelstoke has everything an adventurous pack could want: long powdery winters and warm, radiant summers.

In spring, the hills around the valley shed their snowy capes to make way for meadows of wildflowers; lakes thaw to invite summer sports; and hiking trails become visible. "We camp a lot, and most campgrounds up here allow dogs," Niki observed. "A favorite place of mine is Blanket Creek, which is about twenty minutes out of Revelstoke along Highway 23 South. The views in this area will never disappoint!" While camping here you can visit the manmade swimming lagoon, hike the nearby trails, and even visit scenic Sutherland Falls. Another great place to visit is Martha Creek Provincial Park along the shores of Lake Revelstoke, which can be found along Highway 23 North. This park has easy lake access, and vistas of evergreen hills hugged by clouds. "Holy moly, it's beautiful there," enthused Niki. Be sure to take the dog-friendly hiking trail across the highway.

"We spend a lot of time outdoors along the Columbia River where you can go swimming (but the glacier water is cold!)," Niki continued. "You can hike trails, have a picnic, and spend time with family . . . it's truly an incredible place to be. The dogs get to have this freedom they don't normally have. They can generally be off-leash and swim and dig and explore and just experience pure joy."

Mount Revelstoke is the peak for which the community gets its name, and a major attraction for visitors. Dogs are restricted in several areas, but the Meadows in the Sky area permits pets on-leash. "It's a massive meadow of wildflowers on top of a mountain, and just the most beautiful hiking area—if you're visiting, it's a must," said Niki.

Revelstoke is an animal lover's paradise, home to cougars, deer, coyotes, lynx, bobcats, moose, and bears—both black and grizzly. But with an alert mindset and some cautionary measures, you and your dog can share the woods safely. "Most animals do their thing, and if you're nonthreatening, they generally just carry on past you," Niki said. "The bears tend to have routines. We have one fellow who comes by to the river, right into town, gets a drink, then walks back into the hills. He mostly keeps to himself. You get used to it." If you're hiking in one of the national parks, you might see a trail that's been closed off by the park staff because a bear has been spotted sleeping nearby. But if you're hiking outside of the areas managed by the park service, it's especially important to be prepared, and to carry bear spray and know how to use it.

"One time I was out hiking in a mountain range a little further out from Revelstoke," continued Niki. "I had eight or nine dogs with me, and we got surrounded by a pack of wolves. I knew they were wolves because they sound very different from dogs or coyotes, and they are much bigger. The pack was just up the trail from us. And my dogs, all of them, came to a slow stop, until they were standing silently around me. It was like they knew 'Okay, this is not a coyote or a deer . . . this is serious business!' Not one of them wanted to interact—they knew it was a dangerous situation. Then we all slowly turned around and went back.

"The nice thing about Revelstoke is there are trails everywhere. So if one hike is simply not in the cards for you that day, it's very easy to find another."

For visitors wishing to avoid wildlife encounters, the 3.1-mile Begbie Falls hike near downtown Revelstoke is a great choice. "You can hike down and have a picnic at the waterfall and then hike back up. Kids and dogs can play in the water; you can explore and have fun with your whole family. It's a beautiful way to spend a day."

Summertime in the town Revelstoke has its own rugged charm. On Saturday evenings, live music is usually heard bouncing off the brick facades, and local farmers' markets pop up on the cobblestone streets, selling local produce, jewelry, and prepared foods. "Half of Revelstoke is down there getting their vegetables in the summer, and of course dogs are welcome," said Niki.

Before heading out for a day of adventure, visitors can fuel up at the Modern, a café on MacKenzie Avenue (the tiny town's main street), for coffee and not-to-be missed pastries. The pet-friendly outdoor seating area has a breathtaking view of the mountains.

"It's really nice to live in a place where everybody seems to have a dog, and dogs can be let out, and play, and explore," Niki concluded. "I think this is a really beautiful place to be a dog."

NIKI PERRY is a board-certified professional dog trainer (CPDT-KA), canine behavior consultant (CBC), and Karen Pryor Academy Certified Training Partner (KPACTP). On a daily basis, she works with animals that are struggling emotionally, physically, and within their soul essence. Her approach to helping them heal takes consideration of the whole body and all the intricate systems that make it function optimally. Niki has spent the past twenty years educating herself, and is also a certified equine massage therapist, a Reiki practitioner, canine herbalist, pet food nutrition specialist, and an essential oils practitioner. She is also a wife, a proud mother of two kind and courageous girls, and a stepmom to a wonderful young man. Niki's family, which also includes two dogs and a senior cat, currently resides in the beautiful town of Revelstoke, British Columbia.

If You Go

▶ **Getting There:** The closest airport, Kelowna, is two and a half hours away from Revelstoke by car. Visitors can also consider flying to Calgary, which is a larger airport but four hours' drive from Revelstoke.

▶ **Best Time to Visit:** Revelstoke's hot, sunny summers are perfect for hiking, and the long, powdery winters appeal to snow sport lovers.

▶ **Accommodations:** Revelstoke is a resort town with a large number of dog-friendly hotels and vacation rentals. Visit seerevelstoke.com for details.

▶ **Supplies:** The main pet store in town is Animal House (250-837-5956).

VANCOUVER

RECOMMENDED BY **Sébastien Dubois**

Vancouver, tucked into the southwest corner of the Candian province of British Columbia, is easily one of the most beautiful cities in North America. The city center is bordered by water on three sides—Burrard Inlet to the north, False Creek to the south, and English Bay to the west. On its northern tip is Stanley Park, one of North America's largest urban green spaces. The North Shore Mountains are in view on all but the foggiest days, further enhancing the city's natural beauty. Long the commercial center of British Columbia, Vancouver boasts a diverse and cosmopolitan community (including Canada's largest Chinatown) that now attracts nearly ten million tourists a year.

"Before my partner and I got our golden retriever, Bruno, I was the guy stopping and admiring every dog I passed on the street," Sébastien Dubois began. "In the year and a half since Bruno came to live with us, I'm now the one being stopped; everyone wants to pet the head of a nice golden retriever. Vancouver always seemed to be a dog-friendly city, but since we've had Bruno, I've become part of the dog community and see how important dogs are to Vancouverites. Thanks to Bruno, we know everyone in our building—a building on the city's west end that we moved to so we could be closer to Stanley Park—and we've made many relationships in the neighborhood with other dog owners."

Two of the city's greatest outdoor assets—Stanley Park and the Vancouver Seawall—are a boon to both dogs and their owners. Stanley Park encompasses more than one thousand acres—the northwestern half of the city's downtown peninsula. Its amenities include fifteen-plus miles of forested trails, a par-3 golf course, a pool, a water spray park, an aquarium, a miniature railway, beaches, a lake, an outdoor theater, a few restaurants, and five and a half miles of the Vancouver Seawall. The seawall has been called "the world's longest uninterrupted waterfront path," and extends from Coal Harbor on the

city's north side, around Stanley Park to English Bay, and then around False Creek on to Kitsilano Beach. The seawall is divided into two sections: The half closest to the water is reserved for walkers and joggers, the inside path for bikers and inline skaters.

"For many dog owners, Stanley Park is the go-to spot, whether on the seawall or the hiking trails," Sébastien continued. "One walk we like to do with Bruno is from Second Beach to Lovers Walk Trail, then on to Beaver Lake, the Rose Garden, and Coal Harbor. We also like to walk around Kitsilano Beach."

Another unique and rather whimsical facet of Vancouver life is the city's miniature ferries, which spirit humans and dogs alike back and forth across False Creek on the south side of the downtown peninsula. "The ferries are tiny, and can accommodate eight people," Sébastien explained. "They are dog-friendly, and the rides are short, five minutes or so. Again, you get a fabulous perspective of the city and mountains from the boat. Bruno loves to hang his head outside."

A favorite destination for Vancouverites—be it by boat or foot—is Granville Island, which juts into False Creek. Once a blighted industrial area, Granville is now a wonderfully inviting public space. Granville's Public Market features more than fifty food vendors; other island tenants include art galleries, performing arts venues, restaurants, brewpubs, and cafés. "In Vancouver, the regulations are that if food is served, no animals can come inside," Sébastien said. "But since COVID, there are many more patios now, where dogs are allowed. One I like very much is at Alimentaria Mexicana, on Granville Island."

Vancouver has many dog-friendly accommodations. If your pooch (or partner) is deserving of a little special pampering, consider one of the city's Fairmont properties. "Vancouver is the only city with three Fairmont hotels," Sébastien noted. "Every room at each of the properties—the Fairmont Hotel Vancouver, the Fairmont Waterfront, and the Fairmont Pacific Rim—is dog-friendly, with a dog bed, dog food, and treats. While pets can't be left in the room alone, pet sitters are available. At the Fairmont Hotel Vancouver, there are dogs with the concierges." Ella, a Lab/golden retriever mix, and Elly, a black Lab, join their humans (who work at the hotel) five days a week, and are happy to visit with guests.

Sébastien shared how an ideal "dog day" might evolve in Vancouver: "Bruno and I might start the day with coffee and brunch at Greenhorn Cafe in the west end, a very dog-friendly spot. Then we'd head for Stanley Park, walk the trails around the lagoon, and on to Second Beach. From there, we'd walk the seawall back along English Bay toward the city. We might grab lunch at Score on Davie, a popular sports bar. It's not far from there

OPPOSITE: A dog and its human take in the view of downtown Vancouver from Stanley Park, a favorite destination for Vancouverites and their pups.

to Sunset Beach, where there's a grassy patch overlooking False Creek and an off-leash area where Bruno can run and play. From there, we might grab a ferry across to Vanier Park and walk to Kitsilano Beach. Perhaps we'd stop for a snack or pint on Yew Street, which has a number of cafés and pubs. If we're not worn out, we might walk the seawall a bit more to Granville Island before heading home."

Another great way to end a summer day in Vancouver might be a trip to the beach. "Last summer we took Bruno out to Spanish Banks, the beach furthest west of the city," Sébastien shared. "A section of the beach is open to dogs. When the tide is out, you can walk almost a mile out and not be much above your knees. The dogs can run through puddles, roll in the mud, chase after crabs. To the west is the setting sun; to the east, the city in the last light of day."

SÉBASTIEN DUBOIS is the executive director of industry partnerships for Destination Canada. He has deep roots in the tourism sector. His early work as a tour guide shaped his passion for the industry and laid the foundation for future roles with Intrawest, Travelocity, and Expedia. As the sales and market development manager for the Americas at Tourism Vancouver, he gained perspective on tourism's value to the global economy and stretched his approach to bridging cultural and geographic distance. In addition to exploring Vancouver with his golden retriever, Bruno, Sébastien treasures bringing the three generations of his family together to create new memories.

If You Go

▶ **Getting There:** Vancouver is served by most major carriers.

▶ **Best Time to Visit:** Vancouver generally experiences a temperate, if moist, climate, not unlike Seattle's. The most reliably dry weather comes from June through September.

▶ **Accommodations:** You'll find a partial list of dog-friendly lodging options at destination vancouver.com. The three Fairmont properties in town come well recommended (800-257-7544; fairmont.com).

▶ **Supplies:** There are many pet stores in downtown Vancouver, including Spoiled Paws (604-899-1220; spoiledpaws.ca).

WHISTLER

RECOMMENDED BY **Sarah McMillan**

Like so many visitors before her, Sarah McMillan came to Whistler for a season . . . and not long after, pulled up stakes from Northern England to make Whistler her home. "It's such an awesome place to be in general, and it's especially dog-friendly," she enthused. "There are trails that connect all the parts of town, so you really don't need to have a car. There's something special about every season: In the winter, there's snowshoeing, cross-country skiing; in the spring and summer, biking, hiking, and the chance to get out on area lakes; in the fall, you have the beautiful foliage. I began working for a dog-sitting company after I relocated. A few years later, an opportunity came up to buy the company, allowing me to continue my passion working with dogs."

Whistler sits roughly seventy miles due north of Vancouver in British Columbia's Coast Mountains. The ski resort—North America's largest—has a staggering 8,100 acres of terrain. The region was first recognized for its recreation potential in 1911 by Alex and Myrtle Philip, two transplants from Maine. By 1914, the Philips had established the Rainbow Lodge on the shores of Alta Lake; the lodge was named for the lake's resident rainbow trout. (The town was originally named Alta Lake, but took the name Whistler in recognition of the high-pitched calls of the hoary marmot, a species of ground squirrel endemic to the surrounding mountains.) With the Pacific Great Eastern Railway in place to convey visitors to the lake's shores, the Rainbow Lodge soon became an acclaimed destination for anglers. By the 1920s, it was the most popular summer resort west of the Canadian Rockies. By 1960, plans were afoot to begin development of a ski resort on London Mountain in Whistler, in hopes of attracting the 1968 Olympics. Though that bid fell short, Whistler Blackcomb was eventually visited by the Winter Olympics and Paralympics . . . fifty years after the idea was initially hatched.

Following the example of other leading ski resorts, Whistler took advantage of its spectacular surroundings to develop summer amenities, including a world-class mountain biking park and several award-winning golf courses. These, combined with the rivers, lakes, and mountains provided by nature, have made Whistler a true four-season resort . . . for dogs *and* their humans.

A great place to begin your exploration of Whistler is the Valley Trail, a car-free network of paved trails and boardwalks that link together the town's various neighborhoods, skirting rushing rivers and scenic lakes. The trail's twenty-five-plus miles are open year-round for walkers, runners, cyclists, and skaters; sections are maintained in the winter for walking, cross-country skiing, and fat biking. "You can get pretty much anywhere in Whistler on the Valley Trail," Sarah continued, "and it's very accessible in the winter as well. Most stores en route allow dogs. As you walk along, people will want to give your dog a treat so they can pet him." (Note that black bears are sometimes seen along the Valley Trail, especially in late summer and fall. By keeping your distance, ideally one hundred yards or more, and keeping your dog on-leash, you, your dog, and the ursines that call the woods home should remain safe.) A few favorite walks are A River Runs Through It, which crosses the River of Golden Dreams, then continues to glacier-fed Green Lake and back to its starting point along Fitzsimmons Creek; and Beaches and Boats, which leads to picturesque Alta Lake.

Surrounded by mountains and deep forests of cedar and fir, it's no surprise that greater Whistler offers an abundance of hiking trails; nearby Garibaldi Provincial Park has more than fifty miles of maintained trails alone. One of Sarah and her husky Koda's favorites is Train Wreck. "The trail begins just south of Function Junction," Sarah described. "It takes you through the forest, across a suspension bridge, to the wrecked train cars in the middle of the forest. There are also numerous biking and hiking trails that veer off the main trail." How did the train cars come to be there? According to the Whistler Museum, in 1956, a train derailed on the nearby rail line, and three boxcars were tightly wedged in a canyonlike area. A local logging company was retained to pry the cars free. Once they did, they dragged the boxcars up the tracks and rolled them into the forest, where they remain at rest, though now brightly decorated with graffiti. "Koda really likes the Train Wreck, as it's surrounded by nature and great smells," Sarah added. Other dog-recommended trails include Ancient Cedars, Brandywine Meadows, Riverside, and the complex of paths at Lost Lake Park. "Of course, you can snowshoe up any of the mountains in the winter," Sarah added. "And there are many miles of dog-friendly cross-country trails at Ski Callaghan and the Whistler Olympic Park."

There's nothing like a refreshing swim to cool a woofer off on a warm summer's day. The Whistler region's many lakes provide ample swimming opportunities. The Canine Cove dog beach at Lost Lake, just a fifteen-minute walk from town on the Valley Trail, is a favorite off-leash dog area where dogs can splash about. Another is at Alpha Lake Park (known locally as "Arfa" Lake), where a dock makes for great lake leaps. (There's also an adjacent off-leash park.)

"Taking your dog out on a lake on a stand-up paddleboard makes a great memory," Sarah mused. "After all, dogs are instinctually at home out in nature, and super happy to share that time with their human."

At the dimming of the day, it's a pleasure to unwind with a cold beverage. Whistler offers several fine options. "We have two breweries with dog-friendly patios, Whistler Brewing and Coast Mountain Brewing," Sarah added. "Both are very good, locally owned, and there are always a few woofers about."

SARAH MCMILLAN grew up in Newcastle, England. She traveled the world by working on cruise ships, and eventually landed in British Columbia. It felt like home, and she stayed. Sarah started working as a dog walker with Whistler Dog Sitting (whistlerdogsitting .com) and eventually bought the company, which she currently operates.

If You Go

▶ **Getting There:** Most visitors fly into Vancouver, which is served by most major carriers. From Vancouver, Whistler is a two-hour drive; bus and train transfers are available.

▶ **Best Time to Visit:** While Whistler is a winter sports mecca, many canine visitors (and their people) like to visit in the summer season, from mid-June through September.

▶ **Accommodations:** Tourism Whistler (whistler.com) lists a variety of dog-friendly lodging options.

▶ **Supplies:** Happy Pets near Function Junction has most of your dog needs covered (604-932-3050; facebook.com/WhistlerHappyPets).

DESTINATION

10

MARIN COUNTY

RECOMMENDED BY **Trish King**

The cluster of demure, leaf-shaded towns just north of the Golden Gate Bridge have a reputation that often precedes them. Marin is one of the wealthiest counties in the nation, and also one of the greenest, with Muir Woods National Monument, Point Reyes National Seashore, a burgeoning farm-to-table food scene (much of the west county is farmland), and over 249 miles of hiking trails, all within the county's boundaries.

"I came here because I was a hippie!" recalled Trish King. "I came for the summer love. Initially I worked in radio. But what I do now is far more interesting. And far more cuddly."

Marin County is a proudly canine-centric community. Walk down the shady, European-inspired sidewalks of San Anselmo's Center Boulevard, and you'll notice virtually every bookstore, café, and boutique has a water bowl outside and a treat waiting. Mill Valley's sun-dappled, ivy-lined downtown has numerous parks where dogs can be seen frolicking under hundred-year-old redwoods, lapping up a drink at the fountains in front of Depot Café and Bookstore, or simply strutting down Miller Avenue, taking in the boutique shopping with their owners. There are over twenty-five pet groomers in the county, ten stores that specialize in holistic and raw dog food, and a countless number of dog-friendly hiking trails.

"Blithedale Ridge is one of my favorite morning walks," Trish said. "It's between Corte Madera and Mill Valley, three miles long, relatively flat, and still somehow has relatively few people. Another place I tend to go is Indian Valley, in Novato. It's very pretty, very flat, and a great place to be social with other dogs. You pass people, and everyone says hello."

A network of wide, paved fire roads weaves through the forests that provide the rich green frame to all of Marin's towns. You can hop onto a hiking trail in the redwood-

OPPOSITE:
A large network of trails cross through the lush hills of Marin County, most of which are dog-friendly.

lined streets of Larkspur, jump on a fire road, and, after a pleasant walk that alternates through magical forests and charming downtowns, end up staring at the Pacific Ocean above Sausalito Harbor. Marin County Parks keeps regular lists of trails and fire roads to help you navigate (cell service can get spotty, even today).

"The funny thing is, for a long time, there was no signage saying that you could walk your dog off-leash on the fire roads," reflected Trish. "There was some confusion. I was part of a series of public hearings to decide what to make official. At the same time, I was on the board of the Association of Professional Dog Trainers. We were asking ourselves how many dogs an individual could take off-leash on a trail, with birds and deer and coyotes around. Some people thought none. Some people thought there was no limit. But we settled on three, if you can keep them under voice control. Generally, as soon as you get on the single-track trails, you're supposed to be on-leash— the signs will let you know. We have to realize how privileged we are to be able to walk our dogs off-leash under voice control at all; this isn't common in a lot of places where there is significant wildlife.

"One time I was walking on Blithedale Ridge with Ariel, my Belgian shepherd, and Jo-Bear, my rottweiler," continued Trish. "Then suddenly Ariel disappeared. I thought 'Oh no, where is she?' Then I looked about two hundred feet ahead and suddenly saw her flirting with another dog. I got closer, and I realized it wasn't a dog. It was a coyote. I had a heck of a time getting her back. He was flirting with her, too— she didn't want to leave. Spayed females still like intact males."

A favorite pastime for locals and residents alike is to bundle the family into the car and head west along Route 1, up and over Mount Tamalpais, toward the county's beaches. Small towns along the protected seashore, such as Inverness, Point Reyes, and Bodega Bay, are a marvelous reward for those who can make it down the arrestingly beautiful—and profoundly curvy—coastal roads. If you and your dog are feeling a bit woozy from the drive, pay a visit to off-leash Kehoe, Limantour, Upton, or Dillon Beach in northwest Marin and let the brisk sea breeze refresh you (be sure to bring layers—you never know when the fog is coming back in). "Closer to civilization, Rodeo Beach is a great dog beach up near the Headlands, right across from the Golden Gate Bridge," Trish said. Your dog can play there, and you don't have to drive an hour, and it's not like state parks, where they require a full-time leash or usually forbid dogs entirely.

DESTINATION 11

"Marin is so pretty," Trish concluded. "They have kept the population somewhat contained. There are hills, the fog, the ocean . . . it's got every natural beauty, as far as I'm concerned. Except snow."

TRISH KING is a certified professional dog trainer and certified dog behavior consultant. She established the Canine Behavior Academy at the Marin and Silicon Valley Humane Societies and teaches in-person and online workshops on behavior, canine management, temperament assessment, and handling difficult dogs. Her speaking engagements have included the Association of Professional Dog Trainers, American Humane, as well as CalAnimals' Animal Care Conferences. She is a member of the American Humane Task Force for Humane Dog Training, equipment chair of the Delta Guidelines for Humane Dog Training, member of the task force to restructure PetSmart dog training practices, instructor with Dogs of Course's Instructor Training Courses, webinar instructor with the Association of Professional Dog Trainers and E-Training for Dogs, and telecourse instructor with Raising Canine. She is the author of *Parenting Your Dog*, as well as numerous articles about dog and cat behavior for local and national newspapers and magazines.

If You Go

▶ **Getting There:** Marin County is just about a half-hour drive north of San Francisco International Airport, which is served by a large variety of airlines.
▶ **Best Time to Visit:** Marin is temperate year-round, with mild summers and winters. Spring has wonderful wildflower blooms, when the "golden hills" are transformed to bright green.
▶ **Accommodations:** Vacation rentals are available through a variety of vendors, and a list of dog-friendly hotels is available at visitmarin.com.
▶ **Supplies:** There are countless pet stores, but a favorite local chain with a few stores around the county is Woodlands Pet Food & Treats (www.woodlands.pet).

DESTINATION 11

PALM SPRINGS

RECOMMENDED BY **Steve Piacenza** AND **Jimmy McGill**

There is no shortage of sunny getaways in Southern California, but Palm Springs is where the metropolitan locals often flock to slow down and recharge from the bustle of the city. Palm Springs greets desert travelers with a famous mid-century California aesthetic, complete with palm trees, pink flamingos, and retro-themed hotels. And the family dog is welcome to come along on the holiday.

"Most hotels and Airbnb's are dog-friendly," said Steve Piacenza. "No one would have any trouble finding a place. There're tons of dog parks, and every city park has a wag-bag dispenser. There are also loads of hiking trails. You need to be a little aware and read the signs, as we do have protected bighorn sheep out here. But it's easy to bring your dog out and take them to a park or on a hike." This includes nearly twenty miles of rolling desert hills in the Mission Creek Preserve, or the cool, stark slopes of Whitewater Canyon. Visitors can climb up to a bluff that offers arresting views into the canyon and out onto the high peaks of the San Gorgonio Wilderness.

Although SoCal's notorious summer heat might scare off some tourists, the locals know the truth: Most of the year, the weather in Palm Springs is actually "stunning." In fact, the varied climate can present some interesting contrasts. "In January it's seventy degrees. But the mountains behind me, they are snowcapped," said Jimmy McGill. "So you can go up there, walk in a trail of snow in the mountains, and drive back down, and be lying by the pool in twenty minutes.

"In the summer, of course, it is very hot. You have to get your dog out before seven A.M. or after nine P.M. Temperatures are often one hundred degrees or more, and when you think about the concrete on your dog's paws, that can be around 150 degrees." To compensate, however, there are several locations where you can take shelter from the

OPPOSITE:
The open-air
atrium at
Boozehounds
provides an
inviting space for
dogs (and their
humans) to enjoy
a libation.

broiling desert heat, keeping you and your pup cool and comfortable. Koffi, the dog-friendliest café in town, offers pups an entire outdoor courtyard with year-round green grass, where dogs can cool their paws while their owners sip an iced latte. Restaurants like Farm and the Colony (the flagship eatery of the extravagantly purple Colony Palms Hotel) feature dog-friendly patios. And then there's one restaurant that doesn't just allow dogs, but welcomes them as enthusiastically: Boozehounds.

"I wanted to be able to take my dog somewhere safe, where he could be comfortable during the summer heat," said Jimmy, "and as dog-owners, you kind of get used to just being tolerated when you bring your dog into most places. We had a dream to have a place where you weren't just being tolerated. This isn't where you bring your dog, it's where your dog brings you." Boozehounds opened in April 2021, during the COVID-19 pandemic, but nevertheless has quickly become a local favorite. "We have it divided into three areas: a dining room with a bar—and per California law, there are no dogs in that area—but there are two other sections beyond that dining room. There's the atrium, which is all glass, and the walls and ceilings open up to allow the fresh air in. And then beyond that is a huge patio with a cabana bar," Steve described.

Boozehounds sports a minimalist, mid-century vibe, with palm trees, green velvet couches, and beautiful lighting. Humans can order up a cocktail like the Old Yeller or Aunt Donna's Dirty Poodle before perusing the menu curated by executive chef Aric Ianni, featuring Southern California fare and seasonal ingredients. Similarly, each dog that comes in, whether they're "in a baby carriage or the size of a horse," is greeted with their own tableside bed, a fresh water bowl, and a canine-friendly menu. "We joke that the dogs get served water before the humans do," Jimmy added.

A misconception some may have about Boozehounds—as with Palm Springs in general—is that it would have a cheap or kitschy feeling, a kind of plastic tourism without real holiday comfort. Jimmy said, "We had an incredible brander and designer who kept us in line. In fact, many guests make reservations for our dining room for an amazing night out for cocktails and dining, and they are shocked to learn there may be fifty-plus dogs just yards away in our canine-friendly atrium and patio. It takes a great group of dedicated hospitality experts and dog lovers to make an operation like this successful."

Some people might be concerned about so many different dogs in one space, but one year into their venture, Jimmy and Steve have yet to see any problems. "I think the dogs know what's going on," said Jimmy. "They are so well-behaved. Of course, we also have to attribute this to their responsible human companions. Greeted with love, water bowls, and treats certainly helps our pups feel at home.

"In Palm Springs, you get all these people from Los Angeles and Long Beach, people of all age groups, just exhausted with the big city. We were exhausted with the big city, and so many things changed during COVID. People come here for that specific relaxed lifestyle. That includes your dog. We are really proud to be contributing to that."

STEVE PIACENZA is the cofounder, along with Bryan Rogers and Jimmy McGill, of Boozehounds in Palm Springs. In addition, he owns and operates a production company called Beyond B Entertainment. He produces do-it-yourself programming and is also a DIY host for HGTV and Magnolia Network. He executive produces his own shows and has been nominated for two Emmy Awards. Steve has his own product line of arts-and-crafts merchandise, which can be found at Walmart.

JIMMY MCGILL is the cofounder, along with Bryan Rogers and Steve Piacenza, of Boozehounds in Palm Springs. He created Glitterati Tours, the number one tour company in Beverly Hills. His keen eye on market trends, as well as providing first-class customer service, propelled Glitterati to success in a very competitive tourism market. Prior to his career in hospitality, he worked as a researcher and writer for television in Los Angeles.

If You Go

▶ **Getting There:** Palm Springs International Airport is served by thirteen airlines, with many routes on Southwest (800-435-9792; southwest.com).
▶ **Best Time to Visit:** Winter and early spring are the most popular times to visit, thanks to the temperate weather and chance to see snow on the mountains.
▶ **Accommodations:** Visit Greater Palm Springs lists reliable hotels at visitgreaterpalm springs.com.
▶ **Supplies:** The boutique pet shop Bones-N-Scones (760-864-1133; bonesnscones.com) is a favorite for grain-free and holistic treats.

SAN DIEGO

RECOMMENDED BY **Michele Presley**

Nicknamed "America's Finest City," San Diego is famous for its relaxed atmosphere, 266 days of balmy sunshine, and miles and miles of welcoming beaches—including for your dog. "The first time I came, I liked it so much, I kept extending and extending my stay. I ended up living here for six weeks," remarked Michele Presley. "And the best part is, you can bring your dog just about everywhere. It's that same feeling you have when you to go Carmel. In San Diego, most people have a dog. People are happy to see you with your dog. Being out with your dog is normal. There's this general feeling of warmth and welcoming; you never feel like an outsider for having your dog with you."

The city of San Diego is surrounded by smaller, more intimate communities, including the little town of Del Mar, which boasts what might be the most famous dog park in California. Officially named North Beach, the locals refer to it simply "Dog Beach," and for good reason. "If you were a dog, this would be heaven," said Michele. Located north of Twenty-Ninth Street, Dog Beach stretches to the Solana Beach border, including the mouth of the San Dieguito River. "None of the pictures truly capture it," reflected Michele. "There is every type of dog imaginable, frolicking, greeting one another, playing chase, splashing in the waves. It's an off-leash park, but some more skittish or unpredictable dogs are kept on-leash by their owners, and everyone is very respectful. I never saw a fight, or even so much as crossed words between dogs. And everyone is really good about picking up their pet's waste." The southern and northern sides of the beach are separated by the mouth of the San Dieguito River. When the tide is out, you can walk across, and in most seasons, both sides are open to dogs. In the summer, however, the southern section (also known as Main Beach) tends to be reserved for human visitors only, so be sure to observe any signs before wandering too far down the coast with your pup.

*OPPOSITE:
In San Diego,
dogs can play in
the sand or tackle
the waves on
a surfboard
of their own.*

"There's another dog beach Kismet, my Chihuahua mix, loved in San Diego proper, called Ocean Beach," continued Michele. "The beach itself is smaller than Dog Beach, but there's a dedicated parking lot as opposed to hassle of street parking, and an additional grassy area if your dog tires out from the water quickly. It's quite nice."

If your dog simply can't get enough of the water, consider visiting San Diego when one of the area's many dog surfing competitions is happening. The Surf Dog Surf-A-Thon typically takes place in September, right at Dog Beach, with the winning pooch taking home baskets of treats, premium pet food, toys, and other goodies; the event raises funds for the Helen Woodward Animal Center. Just a few minutes south of San Diego, Imperial Beach hosts the original Surf City Surf Dog competition, where more than sixty dogs compete to raise funds for the San Diego Humane Society. If your dog has never been on a board, or perhaps just needs to brush up before the big day, there are a variety of private dog surfing lessons available from local instructors like SoCal Surf Dogs and Surf Pups, to name just a few.

After working up an appetite in the water (and ensuring we've shaken the ocean out of our fur), finding a place to dine is a pleasant task. "In La Jolla, I was staying at the Hilton Torrey Pines, which like most hotels in the area is fairly dog-friendly," said Michele. "But next door is the Lodge at Torrey Pines, which has the best hamburger on the face of the planet. I'm serious. There's something about it. Maybe it's the bread? I'm not sure. I almost never eat hamburgers and I think I went back three times. And, of course, they have a lovely patio, where you can sit and enjoy with your dog.

"One of my favorite places was called the Presley, which I went to because, well, the name was intriguing," said Michele. "It's at the Point Loma Liberty Station, a wonderfully kept old military park, across from the 52 Boats Memorial. The Women's Museum of California is there (I took Kismet, of course—she's a lady), and it's really not to be missed. Afterward, we went to the Presley, which is this big, open building with multiple levels, and lots of decks and sofas. It's dog brunch paradise. They seated us on our own sofa and served us this incredible brunch at a coffee table. At one point, Kismet got up on the sofa with me, while I was enjoying this incredible rosé, looking at the view, and I remember thinking, 'As a dog person, it doesn't get any better than this.'"

If, for some reason, you need a break from walking your dog on the beach, the in-city dog parks are as friendly as the coastal ones. The most famous is probably Balboa Park, a vast inner-city green space containing San Diego's famous zoo, as well as three dedicated dog parks (within the grounds). "It has a very European feel," described Michele. "You could spend all day just walking around Balboa Park. People come with picnics, play Frisbee, and, of course, there are lots of dogs."

A bit of advice: Although the people of San Diego are reliably dog-friendly, the weather is not always as amiable. "Leaving your dog in the car in the summer months for any amount of time can be lethal," cautioned Michele. "I know most people know this, but in Southern California, even in the spring, the heat is strong. It's something worth mentioning."

Still, Michele concluded, it is well worth the visit. "Out of all the places I've been with my dogs in the country, San Diego really stands out."

MICHELE PRESLEY is a former travel show producer and is now an executive at Tawkify, a matchmaking company based in San Francisco. She rarely leaves the house without her adventurous canine sidekick(s). Over the years, she lived in or visited dozens of US states with her bichon mix, Thor, who navigated airports, subways, restaurants, and business meetings like a pro. Thor passed away in 2020, and she now travels with Kismet, the rescue Chihuahua mix with whom she toured Central and Southern California.

If You Go

▶ **Getting There:** San Diego International Airport is served by numerous carriers, especially Southwest (800-435-9792; southwest.com) and Alaska Airlines (800-252-7522; alaskaair.com).

▶ **Best Time to Visit:** It's best to avoid high summer for your paws' sake. Spring and fall offer wonderful beach weather and more forgiving temperatures.

▶ **Accommodations:** Hotel Indigo in Del Mar (858-755-1501; ihg.com/hotel-indigo) and the Hilton La Jolla Torrey Pines (858-558-1500; Hilton.com) welcome dogs; just be sure to mention it at booking.

▶ **Supplies:** There are dozens of pet shops in San Diego, a continual favorite is Pet Kingdom (619-224-2841; petkingdom.com).

SAN FRANCISCO

RECOMMENDED BY **Jesseca Reddell**

"I always had dogs growing up," Jesseca Reddell began. "As I got older, I started fostering. One of the first dogs I had as an adult I found on Instagram. An account I follow reposted the story of a dog that was in a shelter in Miami. She was super stressed, and when anyone came to visit, she would sit in the back of her kennel and shake. So she didn't have much of a shot. It didn't help that she was a black pit bull–mastiff mix. And this was in a huge, overcrowded, high-kill shelter. I don't know what possessed me to say this, but I wrote, 'If you can get her on a plane out here, I'll keep her.' I didn't have funds for a plane ticket at the time. Long story short, this account started a GoFundMe campaign for followers to contribute for the plane ticket. And by the next morning, it was fully funded. The first time I met Luna, I was picking her up at SFO."

San Francisco is known for its pioneer spirit, from gold chasers to tie-dyed war protestors to start-up dreamers. The City by the Bay also has a long tradition of fierce liberalism and a quintessential empathy for Mother Earth and all her creatures . . . after all, it is named for Saint Francis of Assisi, patron saint of animals. To have a dog as part of your family is completely normal, and taking your dog out is considered as standard as taking your children out.

On the city's north end, be sure to check out the Marina Green and Crissy Field. Off-leash dogs can bound to their heart's content in on the grassy fields, or the family can settle in with a picnic to watch the Golden Gate Bridge float above the sparkling bay as kiteboarders cut hither and thither. Nearby in the posh Marina district, consider a visit to Delarosa. This Italian spot has large outdoor seating areas, and it's not uncommon to catch a designer breed enjoying his own chair at the table.

No trip to San Francisco would be complete without at least one stop in Golden Gate Park, which begins at the eastern end of the former hippie haven Haight-Ashbury and spans more than one thousand acres of trails, botanical gardens, ponds, and museums. There are four dedicated off-leash areas, and dogs are welcome on-leash just about everywhere else. If you happen to visit on a Monday night, head to Zazie in the nearby Cole Valley neighborhood. The staff doesn't just welcome dogs with treats—they'll give you $10 off a bottle of wine if you bring your pup to their spacious patio.

Golden Gate Park terminates on its western end at Ocean Beach. As you make your way west, consider a stop by Devil's Teeth Baking Company in the Sunset district; they make their own dog treats in house (in addition to delicious baked goods for humans). Ocean Beach is where the city meets the expanse of the Pacific Ocean, and dogs are welcome off-leash under voice control.

Although Ocean Beach, the founding site of Burning Man and many other counterculture events, may be San Francisco's most famous shoreline, and the site of many happy doggy playdates, a bit farther south, there is a more impressive dog-friendly attraction that visitors should be sure not to miss.

"Fort Funston was the first place I took Stella, my second rescue dog, out to the beach," Jesseca said. "You park at the top of a cliff, and the path going down is a bit steep, but the view is amazing; you're walking down a cliff right in front of the Pacific Ocean, with ice plant growing all along the cliffside. Then once you get down there . . . the beach is about twenty minutes from one point to the other, and unlike Ocean Beach, you don't see a lot of surfers or swimmers. Occasionally you'll see a hang glider, or some kites in the sky on the weekend. When it's clear, sometimes you can see dolphins and seals playing past the breakers. But mostly it's just people and their dogs. On a weekend, there are probably fifteen to twenty people there, and a handful more or less dogs. But during the week, you get very little traffic." There's a chance your dog will be immortalized, as Fort Funston is also a famous site for photographers, given its superb light.

"Fort Funston was the first time Stella was off-leash in a public area," reflected Jesseca. "She was a bit tentative. She had basically been raised under a house; she had no social skills. It was Luna, really, who taught Stella how to be a dog, because she had been through so much of the same thing. So the waves would come in, and then go out, she would walk up to where the wave had come up, and then sniff it, and look a bit perplexed, and then the wave would start to come in, and she'd sprint back to the sand. And then she'd run back in again once another wave came in."

"San Francisco is pretty famous for its dog-friendliness," Jesseca concluded. "I know people who live in the neighboring counties, who go to San Francisco just to take their dogs there."

One last tip: Be sure to always dress in layers when you're out in San Francisco; if "Karl the Fog," the city's friendly weather pattern, decides to pay a visit, temperatures can plummet.

JESSECA REDDELL is a San Francisco Bay Area–based dog walker and adopted mom to Stella, Buckets, Jade, and Tiny. Jesseca enjoys fostering dogs who need a little extra socialization and love before finding their forever homes. She is also an ex-evangelical who uses her online platform to help others recovering from high-demand religion by making scholarship more accessible to a broad audience. Her followers have dubbed her "the Heathen Queen," and she can be found by that handle on YouTube and @queenoftheheathens on TikTok.

If You Go

▶ **Getting There:** San Francisco is served by most major carriers. From the airport, the Bay Area Rapid Transit (BART) system will take you straight into the heart of the city.

▶ **Best Time to Visit:** The city has mild weather year-round. May through August is the tourist season, despite the foggy (and occasionally chilly) weather. Consider visiting in early fall, which can often be warmer than July.

▶ **Accommodations:** The Hilton Union Square (415-771-1400; hilton.com) welcomes dogs if mentioned at booking. San Francisco's start-ups invented the vacation rental industry, and there are countless dog-friendly apartments for rent throughout the city.

▶ **Supplies:** There are pet stores in every neighborhood, but a city favorite is Village Pets & Supplies (ilovevp.com).

DESTINATION 14

YOSEMITE

RECOMMENDED BY **Kate Sumser**

DESTINATION **15**

It can be a tricky endeavor to venture into a national park with your dog. The United States' national parks, the protected spaces where you'll find America's most majestic and historically important landscapes, are notorious for their rules about furry friends, occasionally outright banning them. This is to protect pets and wild animals alike, preventing unnatural predation and disease transmissions.

Luckily for pet owners, Yosemite National Park, a UNESCO World Heritage site and the crown jewel of the West Coast park system, has found a way to strike the balance between keeping pets, owners, and wildlife happy.

"I had just adopted Luna, a pit bull mix, and we were planning a trip to Yosemite," Kate Sumser recalled. "At first, we weren't sure we could even make it happen, as I know not all national parks are dog-friendly, but I thought, 'Wherever I go, she goes,' and was committed to figuring it out. Turns out, it was completely possible. We stayed a night at a pet-friendly hotel outside the park and then actually camped within the park at a pet-friendly campground. So Luna and I got to experience Yosemite for the first time together."

All drive-in, non-group campgrounds in Yosemite National Park welcome dogs on-leash, and a network of paved paths weave through the park's famous valley, allowing you to see nearly all the most iconic viewpoints with your dog by your side. Generally speaking, if the path is paved, you can take your pup, making it possible to experience Yosemite's spectacular geography with your dog in a safe environment. "We ended up taking a path that led in what felt like the middle of nowhere," Kate continued. "No one else was around, and getting to play on some boulders and see a real slice of Yosemite by ourselves, I felt incredibly fortunate. All the paths were well marked and really clean."

A half mile away from a signed parking area awaits the thundering Bridalveil Fall, popularized by legendary photographer Ansel Adams. The mist from the waterfall can get you surprisingly wet, so be sure to bring a jacket for yourself and any pups who prefer to stay dry. Another physically easy but visually breathtaking hike leads visitors to Lower Yosemite Fall, past incredible views of the tallest waterfall in North America. In Wawona, a village within the park but just a short drive outside of the main valley, hikers might consider the 3.5-mile Wawona Meadow Loop, which boasts incredible springtime wild-flowers. For those in the market for an all-day excursion where dogs are welcome, consider the lesser-known Chowchilla Mountain Road trail, which starts at the Wawona Hotel Golf Course.

"Our favorite hike was probably Tenaya Lake," reflected Kate. "There were other dogs playing in the water there, and that was the first time Luna had actually gone into the water—any water besides a bath. She waded in really gently. She was so nervous, but then saw all the other humans and dogs were having a good time, and eventually got in with me. It was great to have this experience where she could swim in this beautiful, warm, calm, picturesque landscape. I think that is one of my favorite places on the planet."

For the safety of pets, humans, and wildlife, dogs are prohibited from roaming in official wilderness areas of the park. But if you wish to venture to some of the more challenging trails that lead from the valley floor into the mountains, a few options are available to keep your pooch comfortable while you spend the day apart. Yosemite Hospitality is a kennel service that operates within the park from May through September. (The service requires written proof of immunizations.) Just three miles south of the park's west entrance, Tenaya Lodge offers famously pet-friendly rooms along with pet sitting, walking, and kenneling services. As campground spots in Yosemite can be difficult to snag, especially in the peak summer months, Tenaya Lodge is a double beacon for visitors traveling with their dogs. But it's not the only option. A bit farther out from the park entrance, the gold rush towns of Coulterville, Fish Camp, Midpines, El Portal, Catheys Valley, and Mariposa have plenty of storefront water bowls, pet-friendly patios, and dog-friendly hotels.

For chow time, there are a few choice options within the park if you don't want to cook at your campground. Within the park boundary, Degnan's Kitchen offers up coffee and donuts in the morning, wings and pizza for lunch and dinner. For something faster, the Village Grill is a grab-and-go deli, and you and your dog can enjoy yourselves at their patio tables or at any of the picnic tables across the valley floor.

DESTINATION **15**

OPPOSITE: Yosemite is one of a handful of American national parks that has great trails for dogs.

"They seemed pretty open to dogs being there, in general, so long as you are following the rules," Kate continued. "And of course the rules are there for everyone's safety, so they are easy to follow. But even with all the rules, there is something about being able to walk around in the little village in the center of Yosemite Valley. I didn't feel stigmatized for having Luna with me. I didn't feel like I was in trouble. I don't think I was expecting that."

If you want to take your pup on a longer hike than the paved paths available within the park boundary, it's worth noting that Yosemite National Park is surrounded on all sides by national forests—which have significantly fewer dog restrictions. West of the park entrance, consider the Hite Cove trail in Mariposa, where the hills sprout carpets of poppies in the spring. On the east side of Yosemite, head to the ski town of Mammoth, which in the summer boasts the scenic Minaret Lake trail and the Duck Pass Trail to Barney Lake, both long, challenging hikes that reward visitors with magnificent vistas of the east slope of the Sierra Nevadas.

"There are a lot of parks and forests I won't take Luna to, where we wouldn't be welcome or I would worry she wouldn't be comfortable," Kate reflected. "But with Yosemite and that whole area, I can't wait to go back. It was so much fun."

KATE SUMSER is set to graduate law school in December 2022, with the hope of becoming a public defender. Kate spends as much of her free time as possible exploring the world with her dog, Luna. They go to lakes, beaches, hiking trails, and dog parks whenever they can. When they're not out exploring the world, Luna and Kate are often found playing in the yard and trying out new treats for Luna. Adopting Luna was the best decision Kate ever made.

If You Go

▶ **Getting There:** Fresno Yosemite International Airport is served by a handful of airlines, including Alaska Airlines (800-252-7522; alaskaair.com) and American Airlines (800-433-7300; aa.com). You can also fly into Oakland or San Francisco and rent a car for the roughly four-hour drive to Yosemite.

▶ **Best Time to Visit:** Peak season (and the best weather) is May through September. The park service sometimes requires permits for driving into the park between six A.M. and four P.M. that must be reserved ahead of time. If you have a campground reservation within the park, no extra permit is needed. If you are staying outside the park boundary at a dog-friendly accommodation, check with the park service if you need an additional permit to enter the park.

▶ **Accommodations:** Campsites are reservable through the National Park Service, and Yosemite National Park Vacation and Lodging (888-413-8869; travelyosemite.com) has a list of reliable hotels and cabin rentals.

▶ **Supplies:** There are no pet stores inside Yosemite, although the Village Store may stock a limited amount of dog food. Steve's Pet Shop (559-683-5222; stevespetshop.com) in nearby Oakhurst has a more robust collection of food, toys, treats, and gear.

15

DESTINATION

BRECKENRIDGE

RECOMMENDED BY **Camille Presley**

"The thing I really love about Colorado is how many beautiful little pockets there are, little hidden gems in the mountains and along the highways," Camille Presley began. "I had heard about Breckenridge as this magical place, this winter wonderland. When we arrived, I immediately saw that it lived up to the hype."

Breckenridge is best known as a winter sports paradise. Fresh powder carpets the surrounding mountains from November through mid-May—one of the longest snow seasons of any town in the United States. Most ski-in/ski-out lodges welcome dogs as the norm, and trained canines can ride the slopes alongside their human companions.

Even non-skiers will want to visit the majestic Breckenridge Ski Resort, where dogs are welcome to join their owners on the (free) gondola for an impressively scenic ride up to the top of the ridge. The gondola runs winter through summer. Board from the lodge in the center of town, then glide above the Cucumber Gulch Wildlife Preserve, home to elk, moose, deer, and mountain lions. The gondola stops at Peak 7 and Peak 8, where pets and humans can roam about and take in the incredible vista of the town below. (Keep in mind that dogs are not allowed down into Cucumber Gulch itself in an effort to not disturb the endangered boreal toad. But this is one of the few places in and around town where they are forbidden.)

Downtown Breckenridge is a picturesque village of frontier-style log cabins, preserved Victorian homes, local craft boutiques, and distinguished restaurants. "The downtown has done a lot to foster the vibe of a charming mountain town," Camille continued. "It's an oasis from the wild hills, but also has more to do than some of the other small mountain towns in Colorado. All interests are accommodated: hiking, skiing, shopping, fine dining. You don't see a lot of mountain towns that have this much diversity in what they offer."

OPPOSITE:
The Breckenridge
region offers
four-season
recreational
opportunities, all
with sensational
views.

Breckenridge is also rich with American pioneer characters. History buffs can visit the meticulously preserved Victorian home of Barney Ford, a man born into slavery in 1822 who would eventually rise to become one of Colorado's most prominent business-men. Other notable early residents include Edwin Carter, a gold miner turned environ-mentalist and taxidermist, whose collection of almost 3,300 Rock Mountain fauna speci-mens (on display at his museum on Ridge Street) formed the original collection of the Denver Museum of Nature & Science.

In summer, the snow melts and the mountains transform from a skier's paradise into a hiker's haven. "Aside from Cucumber Gulch, ever other trail in Summit County is dog-friendly," continued Camille. "Between the town and the nearby national forest, hundreds of miles of trails are open for humans and dogs. It is usually better to keep dogs on-leash, to prevent any unsavory interactions with wildlife, but this is not always required—just check the signs at the trailhead and bring a leash just in case." Some local favorites include McCullough Gulch, a 6.4-mile trail that leads through rocky slopes, past waterfalls, snow-capped peaks, and crystal clear ponds. Another favorite is the Mayflower Lake route, which meanders through meadows and evergreens before ending at one sparkling lake (it's also a great snowshoeing trek in the winter). For history buffs, the Sallie Barber Mine and Minnie Mine trails are short, easy treks that allow hikers to marvel at abandoned mining sites.

After working up an appetite, dogs are welcome at most establishments back in town. While state laws prohibit non-service dogs from entering indoor-dining establishments, many eateries still welcome pets on the patio and provide custom goodies for visiting pooches. Cool River Coffee House and Clint's Bakery are both known for their home-made dog treats.

"A favorite place we went was Breckenridge Distillery," Camille said. "They have a large outdoor patio that's perfect in the summer, and little doggy cookies out for pups right when you walk in. It's extremely welcoming."

Most stores along the main downtown square allow well-behaved dogs inside, and many have their own shop dog ready to say hello. Consider a stop to Peak-A-Boo Toys, with a massive selection of treats, squeaky toys, and Chuckits, or For Pets' Sake Thrift Store, which offers everything from clothing and housewares to books and art, and all purchases benefit Animal Rescue of the Rockies.

"Something else to keep in mind is that Breckenridge is just off Interstate 70 in Colorado, which is incredibly scenic," continued Camille. "A fun thing to do, if you're coming from Denver, is make it into a little road trip, and enjoy some of the other towns along the route. We stopped at Golden on the way to Breckenridge, and it's precious. The downtown was incredibly charming and quite dog-friendly. They have preserved Victorian villages you can tour, homes, and farms with chicken coops. It's a perfect spot to take an afternoon walk and grab a bit of lunch. We particularly enjoyed a Nepalese place called the Sherpa House, which is a restaurant and cultural center. The food was amazing, and they were very welcoming to all the pups on the patio.

"About a half hour past Breckenridge is another town called Silver Plume. It's a pre-served gold-mining ghost town with tons of character. It's very rustic and rugged, like any minute you'll see two cowboys pop out of a bar and have a John Wayne movie–style shoot-out. Seeing the dogs run downtown, past the Old West buildings, felt very nostalgic, almost like we were watching them running back in time."

If you do go to Silver Plume, be sure to pop into the Bread Bar, a vintage building with great cocktails, and fun music. "They let us take our pups inside and also gave us a tour of the underground cellar," Camille said. "It was another experience like I'd gone back in time.

"In all of these little towns, everyone was very welcoming to us and our dogs," Camille concluded. "You go to some places and you feel like when people see you coming they think, 'Oh God, there are the dog people.' But you don't get that feeling here. The whole time we were there, even the dogs seemed like they were smiling and happy. It felt like they were on vacation, too."

CAMILLE PRESLEY is a Culinary Institute of America–trained chef and a graduate of Ole Miss. Since she was a child, dogs have influenced her personality in more ways than she can count. A constant wanderluster, she has called more than five states home, and has always found comfort in transitions through her connectivity with dogs. From Molly, her childhood dog in Mississippi, she learned to find joy and excitement in her surroundings. In California, from her dogs, Thor and Kizzy, she learned how to be loyal in her relation-ships and stay firm in her beliefs—even if that meant picking just the right French cheese. From Bear in Colorado, she learns daily how to find the good in all and to love the people around us. Camille currently lives in Denver.

16

DESTINATION

If You Go

▶ **Getting There:** Denver International Airport is the easiest entry point to scenic Interstate 70 East, and is served by most major carriers.

▶ **Best Time to Visit:** The snow season is reliable from December to April; hiking trails open up by June and tend to close in October.

▶ **Accommodations:** Breckenridge Ski Resort is bookable year-round (800-789-7663; breckenridge.com), and a number of private apartments and other hotels can be booked through the Breckenridge Tourism Board at gobreck.com.

▶ **Supplies:** There are a few pet shops in Breckenridge's little town, but a favorite is Animal Lover's Pet Supply (970-423-6940; frommfamily.com/r/4252).

COLORADO SPRINGS

RECOMMENDED BY **Krista Heinicke**

In the nineteenth century, Colorado Springs rose to fame as a resort town on the frontier of the American West. The dry climate and fresh mountain air were believed to strengthen the constitution and help heal the lungs. The city was further enriched by two gold rushes (Cripple Creek and Pike's Peak), and railroads clamored for the rights to import tourists and workers. Entrepreneurs like Spencer Penrose and Winfield Scott Stratton donated land and funding for parks and created nonprofit organizations to help them stay preserved. Today, Colorado Springs remains a rustic getaway for artists, history buffs, and nature enthusiasts—and their four-legged companions.

"I moved to Colorado Springs in 1988," Krista began. "The population here has nearly doubled since then, as people crave more outdoor access and desire less and less to be in the city. Colorado Springs is the best of both worlds, in that sense. You have the benefits of a big city, but we're a small mountain town. The Broadmoor area, before it was annexed, was a small village at the foothills of the Rockies and most namely Cheyenne Mountain. When you arrive, be ready to have a good time with your dog."

One of the most notable fixtures of Colorado Springs is the Broadmoor, an expansive and plush 784-room hotel that was once its own proper township, complete with a fire station and post office. "Over the years, I've been able to see its growth from a little hamlet to being part of Colorado Springs," reflected Krista. "But it still feels like its own city. It's a fixture in the economy, a destination within a destination. From the food it serves to the labor it hires for painting and cleaning and engineering, everything is kept local.

"For guests with pets, this is a place where you know your dog will be taken care of in every sense of the word. Let the front desk know you have your dog with you, and there will be a bed, water and food bowls, and every other amenity they could need already wait-

ing in the room when you get here. There's a dedicated room service menu for pets, and treats will be hand-delivered."

The hotel's enthusiastic love for canines spans centuries, and was instigated by its founders, Mr. and Mrs. Penrose. "Mrs. Penrose had an affinity for dogs," Krista explained. "Her favorite was a little poodle by the name of Pitty Pat. When her husband died, she moved into the hotel to live full time, and she brought Pitty Pat with her. I think because of this, having your dog with you at the hotel, and in Colorado Springs in general, just became part of the culture. It's the kind of place you're not just tolerated but encouraged to vacation with your pet. Even Freddie, the director of golf maintenance and grounds who oversees all five thousand acres of the property, has Blaze and Fly, his border collies, following him around while he makes his rounds."

Late December is a popular time to visit, when the Rockies are carpeted in fresh white powder and the township is spangled with twinkling lights. The Broadmoor pulls out all the stops for a picture-perfect Christmas lobby (the pastry chefs have been known to make gingerbread houses the size of race cars). At other times, such as Memorial Day and Fourth of July weekends, visitors can enter their pups into themed pet parades, which also function as fundraisers for local animal charities. "The parades focus on encouraging guests to let their pets strut their stuff around Cheyenne Lake," said Krista. "It's a super-cute event."

No visit to Colorado Springs would be complete without at least a few ventures into the lofty mountains. The entire western border of Colorado Springs acts as an entry point into the Rockies, and the vast network of trails in North Cheyenne Cañon Park and Stratton Open Space welcome dogs on-leash. "The trail system and continuity is huge," enthused Krista. "There's something for everyone and every dog. You can go a quarter mile or several miles. The parks and rec department has been very systematic in trail development and signage, because hiking is such a big part of the culture here. There's nothing better than putting on your hiking boots and getting out there.

"A favorite place to take my dog is Seven Falls. It's one of the most magnificent box canyons around here. You take a paved path down, a little under a mile, and then you're in front of this massive, seven-tiered waterfall. It's breathtaking." At the base of the falls, hikers can choose to continue on to one of three longer hikes, or hop on an elevator for an easy ascent to the top of the falls, where they can take in the arresting view from the observation point.

OPPOSITE:

If your pup tires of pampering at the Broadmoor, there are many dog-friendly trails nearby.

17

DESTINATION

85

Farther northwest of North Cheyenne Cañon Park lies the entrance to Pike National Forest, including several trailheads that lead to the 14,115-foot summit of Pike's Peak (originally named Tava, meaning "Sun Mountain," by the Ute people). Dogs are welcome on the high-elevation trails, although bringing plenty of water is recommended—and keep in mind that dogs can get altitude sickness just as easily as humans. A less-strenuous but perhaps equally magnificent experience can be had at Garden of the Gods Park, a protected geological plain where amber boulders, Great Plains grasses, and southwestern pinon trees collide in a beautiful, quintessentially Coloradoan landscape. Relatively flat and accessible trails weave through the park, and dogs are welcome on-leash.

After working up an appetite, a dog-friendly restaurant can be easily found back in town. "Most of the breweries welcome dogs," Krista noted. "Cerberus Brewing Company is particularly dog-friendly (as you can guess from the name) in their beer garden and outdoor tent. Edelweiss, a German restaurant, also allows pets in their garden. And then, of course, there's, Pub Dog Colorado—the first and possibly only restaurant in the state to allow you to dine indoors with your dog.

"When you have a well-trained pet, they are the best traveling companions," Krista concluded. "The nice thing about this place is that you really get to see your pet enjoy your vacation as much as you do. It's like it's theirs, too."

KRISTA HEINICKE is the director of public relations for the Broadmoor. Her familiarity with the Broadmoor extends to 1984, when she came to Colorado Springs to train for ice dancing at the original Broadmoor World Arena. Prior to working at the hotel, Heinicke co-owned Chez Pierre and has lived in the Broadmoor area since 1989. She is a graduate of the University of Colorado at Colorado Springs, and loves writing about Colorado Springs Wilderness Experiences and hiking with her family of goldens.

If You Go

▶ **Getting There:** Colorado Springs' municipal airport hosts a handful of domestic routes, especially on Southwest (800-435-9792; southwest.com). Visitors can also fly into Denver, then rent a car for the roughly hour-long drive to Colorado Springs.

▶ **Best Time to Visit:** Come in December for unforgettable winter holiday decorations. Hiking season, especially on high-altitude trails, is year-round.

▶ **Accommodations:** The Broadmoor accepts reservations year-round (800-755-5011; broadmoor.com).

▶ **Supplies:** There are pet toys and treats at various shops at the Broadmoor, or you can check out the nearby Pet Pantry & Dog Wash (719-629-9274; pet-pantry.com).

17

DESTINATION

PRAGUE

RECOMMENDED BY **Gigi Chow**

"I've always been drawn to Prague's mesmerizing mix of architecture, especially their dreamy gothic cathedrals, baroque castles, and the medieval Charles Bridge," began Gigi Chow. "Interestingly enough, Prague is also famous for its Cubist and Art Nouveau buildings, which create a unique eclectic atmosphere."

Nicknamed the City of a Hundred Spires, Prague is a mecca for architecture and history buffs, with nearly every architectural style on display, from the delicate details of Saint Vitus Cathedral to the surrealist glass waves of the Dancing House. "Besides the architecture," continued Gigi, "the real reason I brought Roger Wellington [her rescued Yorkshire terrier] to Prague is because I saw the way dogs were allowed inside most of the restaurants and bars. That is one of those factors that really makes the 'hassle' of traveling with your dog worthwhile."

In Prague, the cultural norm is to allow dogs inside virtually every pub, café, restaurant, and shop. It's so common that in the rare case that pets *aren't* allowed, a sticker will usually be placed on the door to alert customers. "From traditional Czech restaurants to Vietnamese eateries, I've never had to ask if I could bring Roger Wellington inside, nor was I ever given any nasty or confused looks while walking in," Gigi reflected. "Sightseeing with him was easy-peasy, and we frequently came across other dog travelers (usually from other European countries, and occasionally from North America like us) so it's rare you are the only person with a dog along. The exception would be that dogs are usually not allowed inside museums or churches, but they are welcome to explore the buildings' exterior grounds, which are often spectacular."

Some notable attractions include the grounds of Prague's ninth-century castle, the largest castle complex in the world and the historical seat of power for Holy Roman

OPPOSITE: Like many European cities, Prague has abundant historical elegant parks to enjoy with your dog by your side.

DESTINATION 18

emperors and presidents of Czechoslovakia. From there, walk toward the Charles Bridge, the famous arched stone roadway that connects the Old Town, across the Vltava River, with the rest of the city. Once in the Old Town, you can follow the walk known as the Royal Way to the gothic Powder Gate, where Czech kings once strolled through on their coronation processions.

Farther south is Charles Square, one of the largest public parks in the world. "That might have been Roger Wellington's favorite," said Gigi. "There were so many other dogs to meet, and so much room to roam. Petřín Hill is also a popular area for dogs with beautiful views of the city at the summit.

"Aside from those sites, I highly recommend visiting Malá Strana, or Lesser Town, with your dog. It's a gorgeous hillside neighborhood that makes for a wonderful area to relax and explore together. It's definitely less touristy, compared to Old Town, which means less foot traffic and a more stress-free walking environment for dogs. The best part is that it offers amazing views across the Vltava River to Old Town. Roger Wellington loved walking along the river here and meeting other furry Czechs on the way. The famous John Lennon Wall covered with graffiti art and Beatles' songs lyrics is also in Malá Strana."

Since dogs are generally allowed inside restaurants in Prague, it's hard to pinpoint a favorite. For a bowl of tasty goulash or a plate of *knedlíky* (Czech dumplings), be sure to stop by Pivovarsky Dum, a traditional Czech restaurant with a microbrewery in the New Town neighborhood. Nearby, the underground music club and bar Vzorkovna (also known as "Dog Bar") has their very own in-house pup, often roaming or catching a nap.

"It's really hard to point out particularly dog-friendly places, since the culture is so pet-friendly overall," Gigi said. "I was once immediately handed a free bottle of cold water by a souvenir shop owner in Old Town after I told him that my dog was thirsty but didn't have the cash to make the purchase. Unfortunately, the store didn't take credit cards and I was out of koruny since I was leaving the next day. At the time, Roger W. was outside with my boyfriend while I went in to find water for him. I usually bring a water bottle for him on outings, but most of it had spilled inside my backpack because I didn't twist it tightly enough. He immediately said, 'Take it!' and then motioned for me to cater to my dog. I said thank you repeatedly and ran off. That really crystallized for me the love and compassion the Czech people have for dogs!"

Getting around Prague by foot is the best way to take in the stunning architecture and immense history. But if you need to catch a bus or train, the good news is, your dog can ride along. "Small dogs are allowed on just about every form of public transportation, as long as they remain inside a carrier or travel bag—dimensions are maxed at 50 × 60 × 80 centimeters," noted Gigi. "In the case of bigger dogs, they must be leashed and muzzled, although enforcement can be a hit or miss.

"One final bit of advice: Like anywhere in Europe, summertime is the peak season for traveling. For the best experience for your dog, I'd say go during spring or fall when there are fewer crowds so you can walk your dog at ease." Gigi concluded. "Plus, you can enjoy some savings on flights and accommodations. It's a huge win-win."

GIGI CHOW left her management job in San Francisco in 2016 to follow her obsession with world travel. As of spring 2022, she has taken her rescued Yorkshire terrier, Roger Wellington, on more than fifty flights, fifteen ferries, and countless trains across more than twenty countries. Their adventures are illustrated through their international dog travel website Wet Nose Escapades: A Yorkie's Guide to Healthy Travel, which is narrated by Roger Wellington himself. Since her ultimate goal is to teach other dog "pawrents" how to travel with their dogs as safely and stress-free as possible, she has authored an e-book called *How to Travel with Your Dog: Roger Wellington's Expert Guide to International Dog Travel*. A huge dog advocate, Gigi can be found advocating for homeless dogs and cats on her travels and writing about humane dog training techniques and dog care tips.

If You Go

▶ **Getting There:** Few international airlines fly direct routes to Prague's Václav Havel Airport, but once in Europe, Ryanair (+44 871 246 0002; ryanair.com) and EasyJet (easy jet.com) supply many different routes.

▶ **Best Time to Visit:** Spring and fall are the best times to avoid the crowds of summer.

▶ **Accommodations:** Most hotels and rentals welcome pets; just be sure to mention your dog when booking. The Prague City Tourism website (www.prague.eu) has a list of many different accommodation types.

▶ **Supplies:** Pet Center (petcenter.cz) is the country's main pet store and has several locations throughout the city.

DESTINATION 18

SANIBEL ISLAND

RECOMMENDED BY **Melissa Halliburton**

"I've always loved animals," Melissa Halliburton began. "I grew up with lots of pets—a rottweiler, two cats, a tortoise, and several lizards. We'd go camping a lot outside of LA as kids, often bringing them all along. But as a young adult, I realized it was actually a huge pain in the butt to travel with my dog, Rocco, a Jack Russell Chihuahua mix. Hotel pet policies weren't published online back then, so you had to call hotel after hotel after hotel to find one that would work. I found it so frustrating that I convinced a dozen friends to help me call every hotel in the country. We created a database of hotel pet policies and used it to launch BringFido. And very soon after, I discovered Sanibel Island."

Sanibel is a mellow, tropical resort town floating off the coast of western Florida. Unlike most islands, it has an east-west orientation instead of north-south. This unique geography results in an unusual amount of large, sandy beaches—which all happen to be dog-friendly. "It has a magical feel to it," continued Melissa. "The minute you cross the bridge (which many people call the 'happy lane'), it feels like you're entering another country, or going back in time. There are no chain businesses, no drive-throughs, no high rises, and no stoplights. Two-thirds of the island is a dedicated wildlife preserve. But also, my favorite thing is that you won't find is any NO DOGS ALLOWED signs. Every single beach and trail on the island is dog-friendly. You just need to keep them on a leash due to the abundance of wildlife: birds, tortoises, lizards, iguanas, snakes, manatees, dolphins, sea turtles, river otters, and, yes, alligators."

Making Sanibel Island such a dog-friendly space was not necessarily the original intent. "If you think about it, the animal protections could have gone another way, especially considering the number of protected bird species." Part of the island's unique dog-friendliness is attributed to Francis Bailey, a legendary businessman, farmer, church

OPPOSITE:
Life slows down
on Florida's
Sanibel Island,
and everyone can
enjoy the break.

builder, justice of the peace, and all-around founding father of Sanibel Island in the 1900s. One of his lifelong goals was to keep the nature of the island as lovely as when he first arrived in 1894. "He was purported to be a big dog lover; his dog was always with him at the store. So I think that had an effect on the dog culture of the island and the sanctuary legislation," noted Melissa.

On Sanibel, humans, dogs, and native species have managed to coexist. "You really would think there would be more problems," reflected Melissa. "But everyone who comes to the island is really respectful. I never see any dog poop on the beach. And some days I don't even see any other dogs on the beach. I think with all the beaches being dog-friendly, there is just plenty of room to spread out. When I had a baby, this was the first place I took him on vacation, too. We rented a tiny cottage right on the beach. Jack was just three weeks old at the time, so my husband and I were barely sleeping. But it was so peaceful. I wasn't worried about Rocco barking at other dogs while my son was sleeping or running into someone who would tell us we couldn't be there, etc. It was the first time I had felt relaxed since my son was born."

Sanibel has no shortage of beaches, and the island is particularly famous for shelling. A favorite spot for uncovering conches, cockles, scallops, and more is Bowman's Beach, a vast stretch of white sand on the island's western side. Farther south, Tarpon Bay awaits kayakers—dogs are allowed on the private rentals that you can obtain from Tarpon Bay Explorers, right on the beach. If you and your dog prefer trails over boats, consider stopping at the J.N. "Ding" Darling National Wildlife Refuge, which takes up most of the island's western side and is nationally noted for its bird-watching. Depending on the season, you can sight nesting ospreys, flamingos, yellow-crowned night herons, and even bald eagles. Dogs are welcome on the Wildlife Drive, Indigo Trail, and Bailey Tract, but they must be kept on a six-foot leash. "There's also a bike trail that loops the entire island," added Melissa. "You can see lots of people riding with their dog in a Burley cart, which you can rent from Billy's Bike Shop."

After a day of adventure (or simply soaking up some Florida sun on the beach), you can catch a bite at one of the island's numerous pet-friendly eateries. Some favorites include Over Easy Café, a brunch spot that is known to give treats to visiting pups, and Island Cow, which even has a dog menu (this beloved dog-friendly restaurant suffered a fire in 2022, but local residents look forward to seeing it rebuilt soon). "I'm also a big fan of 400 Rabbits, Blue Giraffe, the Mucky Duck, and Key Lime Bistro," said Melissa.

Many lodging options on Sanibel are dog-friendly—but there are a few caveats. "Most people who come down are looking for vacation rentals now, and there are tons of pet-friendly ones. The catch is, if you rent a home, you have to stay for a month; that's a city rule. It's an attempt to keep it uncrowded, and have fewer people going in and out on that single bridge." If a longer stay doesn't work for you, hotels allow for shorter stays. "My favorite place is 'Tween Waters Inn, which is directly across the street from the beach and has free kayaks for guests to take out on the Roosevelt Channel (named after a frequent guest). Castaways Cottages and Tropical Winds Motel & Cottages are two other great properties right on the beach.

"I don't tend to repeat trips very often because there are just so many places to explore with my dog," Melissa concluded. "But Sanibel is the kind of place that you just want to go back to over and over again. It is such a serene, welcoming place. Whenever I need to recharge, I go to Sanibel."

MELISSA HALLIBURTON is the founder and CEO of BringFido, the world's largest pet-friendly travel website. Since launching in 2006, BringFido has helped more than one hundred million people take their dogs on vacation. The website includes more than five hundred thousand pet-friendly hotels, vacation rentals, restaurants, parks, beaches, and other attractions in over twenty-five thousand cities worldwide. Halliburton is also the editor and coauthor of the book *Ruff Guide to the United States*, which features 365 of the best places to stay, play, and eat with your dog in all fifty states. When she's not traveling the world in search of new places to feature on BringFido, Melissa can be found on Sanibel Island, where she now lives with her husband, Jason (BringFido's chief operating officer); their son, Jack; and their well-traveled pups, Ace and Roxy.

If You Go

▶ **Getting There:** The largest airport in the area is Southwest Florida International Airport in Fort Myers; carriers include Delta (800-221-1212; delta.com) and Southwest (800-435-9792; southwest.com).

19

DESTINATION

▶ **Best Time to Visit:** Winter is a popular time, as the subtropical temperatures are more mild. If you're coming for bird-watching in the J.N. "Ding" Darling National Wildlife Refuge, consider checking the migration schedules of the species you'd like to see, which vary throughout the year.

▶ **Accommodations:** Tropical Winds Motel & Cottages (239-472-1765; sanibeltropical winds.com) is about a mile from Bowman's Beach. Castaway Cottages (239-472-1252; castaways-cottages.com) is on the very western edge of the island. 'Tween Waters Inn (800-223-5865; tween-waters.com) is just across the bridge from Sanibel on Captiva Island.

▶ **Supplies:** Island Paws (239-395-1464; islandpaws.com) is the main stop for food, treats, toys, and gear.

TAMPA

RECOMMENDED BY **Kathryn Donadio**

The Tampa Bay region is famous for its palm-lined beaches, loyal sports fans, and year-round tropical weather. A calm break from Orlando's theme park crowds, and home to a diverse population thanks to nineteenth-century Cuban, Spanish, German, Italian, and Jewish immigrants who worked in the town's famous cigar industry, Tampa has been slowly climbing the ranks of America's most livable cities. "There's a really nice community feel here," said Kathryn Donadio. "It's very diverse, it's very welcoming, and dogs are everywhere. It has the walkability of a big city, but the feel of a small town. There's been significant investment in the downtown area to connect more neighborhoods. It feels like every person you know has a dog. There's a robust veteran community here, and so there's a large number of therapy dogs and service dogs. Then you have the Dog Moms of Tampa Bay, which puts on a lot of events and meetups."

Some favorite routes include the 2.5-mile River Walk, Tampa's downtown waterfront path that follows the eastern side of the Hillsborough River from the Armature Works mall to Sparkman Wharf. "Sparkman Wharf is a really fun place to take a dog," Kathryn said. It has a large group of restaurants and shops in an outdoor mall of converted shipping containers that creates this fun, outdoor food truck park vibe." It also has shaded and turfed eating areas with spray fans that is especially nice on a hot day. Be sure to also stop by Curtis Hixon Waterfront Park, Tampa's eight-acre dog-friendly festival grounds, complete with splash fountains, a playground, and a dog park. On the other side of the river is Bayshore Boulevard, which holds the title of longest continuous sidewalk in the world. The path weaves south of Tampa's downtown, offering spectacular ocean views along the bay all the way to Ballast Point Park. Dogs can be seen running alongside cyclists, roller skaters, joggers, and walkers, or even gliding down the river on a boat.

"In Tampa, the dog community is very large and extremely friendly," reflected Kathryn. "You can go into most businesses, and they'll give treats out. They have water bowls in the front if your dog needs a drink. Tampa's people understand that dogs are family members, and they're proactive about providing these dog-friendly locations and having places that are accessible to dog owners.

"Another thing about Tampa is that we love our sports teams, and the sports teams really show up for the dog community. The Tampa Bay Lightning have a partnership with Southeastern Guide Dogs. Chris Godwin (the Buccaneers receiver) has the Team Godwin Foundation to help get dogs rescued. You see sports players get involved with charities often, and many are dog-focused."

Catching a game at a pub or brewery is a happy pastime. Tampa has a rapidly growing craft brewery scene, and these pubs are happy to welcome dogs on the patio. One venue in particular, though, caters to a dog's sense of fun almost before that of its humans. "There is no other place in Tampa like Two Shepherds Taproom," said Kathryn. "They are the largest indoor/outdoor dog bar and park in the area. It was founded by a lawyer who wanted to switch careers and got tired of not being able to take his dog out. So he made this pup's paradise. They have splash pads, an outdoor park, and an air-conditioned indoor dog park. For the humans, there are twenty rotating taps, weekly trivia, bingo, and Sunday brunch. You can host a birthday party for your dog, with balloons, decorations, a birthday cake, and everything. During Christmas they do pictures with Santa, which is one of the biggest events of the year—I can't believe how fast the time slots go.

"I remember the first time Shadow, my cattle dog, got into the pool at Two Shepherds. She was confused at first, a little shy. And then she got in, and she was so instantly happy. It just melted me. And the thing I really appreciate about the place is that they keep it safe: They require vaccination records and there's always staff walking around, making sure everyone is playing nicely."

If your dog prefers bigger stretches of water, consider venturing out to explore Tampa's dog beaches. Davis Islands, south of the River Walk, hosts a well-maintained, white-sand dog beach with a wash-off area. Dogs are welcome to run off-leash within the fenced shoreline. Farther out from Tampa and south of St. Petersburg is Fort De Soto Park, a lush, narrow cluster of islands with spectacular beaches. "There's a little forested path that leads out to the dog beach," Kathryn described. "It's another one of those things where at first, Shadow was skeptical, and now she has a blast every time. She loves it.

OPPOSITE:
Splash pads
and water parks
make for happy
dogs on a sunny
day in Tampa.

DESTINATION 20

"There are many people moving into Tampa, and hundreds of dog-friendly places and events," Kathryn concluded. "It really is a community. I knew no one when I moved down here. But if you meet someone with a dog, you're suddenly in this team of dog owners, and all this support and all these connections open up. If you want to be out and about and explore Tampa, you can do that with your dog—the hotels, the restaurants . . . everywhere is accommodating. You don't have to plan separate things. You can explore the city, see what you want to see, and bring your dog along. That's the coolest thing about Tampa Bay."

KATHRYN DONADIO is the founder of @TampaDogs and @DogsofChannelside on Instagram, cofounder and CMO of Dolomites Consulting Group, CEO of Sunshine State Property Group, and founder of Ms Nautica and the Sunshine State of Living lifestyle brands. Kate moved to Tampa Bay from the Baltimore area in 2015 after graduating from college, with honors. She earned degrees in psychology and criminology from Notre Dame of Maryland University, where she held numerous leadership positions, including serving as captain of NDMU's soccer and lacrosse teams. Passionate about helping people reach their goals, Kate has developed a history of success in marketing, training, and consulting for a variety of clients. In 2021, she adopted her cattle dog, Shadow. In her free time, you can find Kate coaching lacrosse, volunteering for veteran and environmental causes, and exploring the outdoors.

If You Go

▶ **Getting There:** Tampa is served by several carriers, especially Delta (800-221-1212; delta.com) and Southwest (800-435-9792; southwest.com).

▶ **Best Time to Visit:** Tampa is tropical year-round, although summers can be particularly hot and fall can bring the occasional hurricane. Winter and spring offer the most temperate weather.

▶ **Accommodations:** Visit Tampa Bay has a list of reliable accommodations at visit tampabay.com.

▶ **Supplies:** A consistent favorite pet shop is Downtown Dogs (813-250-3647; shopdown towndogs.com).

PARIS

RECOMMENDED BY **Carolyn Ryan Healey**

A rallying cry of the French Revolution was *Liberté, égalité, fraternité* ("Liberty, equality, fraternity"). The revolution's proponents were advocating for the human population—though its outcome has ultimately proved beneficial for France's dogs .

"When my family decided to move to Paris with our dog, Lilly [a miniature golden-doodle], and began searching for apartments, I was shocked to learn that landlords are forbidden to discriminate against pet owners," Carolyn Healey began. "It's against the law to disallow pets in apartments. The French love dogs—you see them everywhere. There are leash laws, though the French tend to not keep their dogs on-leash. Overall, they are very well-behaved; they stay right at their owners' feet. Dogs have very wide access to the city as a whole. Many restaurants, especially those with outside seating, are accepting of dogs. Dogs are off-limits at major museums and monuments as well as supermarkets, but they are permitted on the Métro and in doctor's offices, government offices, and many churches, and they're not a problem in outdoor food markets or non-food-oriented stores. I came away from my time in Paris feeling that dogs are built into the infrastructure of both the city and France."

One less savory aspect of dog ownership in Paris, and in France in general, is that people seem less inclined to pick up their puppy's poop, even though waste bags are available near garbage cans in the parks. As a result, the sidewalks can be a minefield. "At least street cleaning vehicles service the roads in Paris on a regular basis," Carolyn pointed out.

It's estimated that Paris is home to over three hundred thousand dogs; that's approximately one dog for every seven Parisians. Given that the average Paris apartment is *intimate* (at least by American standards) and has no terrace or garden access, it's no wonder that Parisians are eager to get their dogs out when schedules permit. (The dogs are likely ready to go, too!) This explains why Paris businesses—especially restaurants and cafés—are so willing to embrace canine guests. As Hazel Smith points out on Bonjour Paris, if one business does not accommodate your pet, the establishment next door will be more than happy to seat both of you—so it's a competitive advantage to be dog-inclusive.

Readers of Ernest Hemingway may come away thinking that Jake Barnes and his patchwork crew of drunken ex-patriots pioneered Paris café culture, as captured in *The Sun Also Rises*. The truth is that cafés were well established two hundred years prior to the novel's publication. "Cafés are omnipresent in Paris," Carolyn continued. "In some neighborhoods, it seems that there is a dozen within a few blocks. There's outdoor seating all year, and many restaurants have outside areas as well. Dogs are always present. Having dogs in the café or restaurant is just an accepted way of life. The French like to linger with their meals; there's such respect for food. Dogs seem to understand this. They relax at meals, too."

Walking—whether to build up an appetite or to help digest your meal post-café—is another time-honored Parisian pastime. Oddly, given the many indoor accommodations afforded dogs in Paris, most of the city's many parks are not open to dogs. But some are. Carolyn shared a few of her favorite dog-walking spots: "I lived in the sixteenth arrondissement, and we'd often head to Jardins du Trocadéro, across from the Eiffel Tower. There's a stunning platform overlooking the Seine. It's a popular spot, with vendors hawking souvenirs, food trucks, and restaurants. There will sometimes be concerts there, and the city will bring out massive screens to televise major sporting events. Nearby, there's the Champ-de-Mars, which used to be used by the French military as training grounds. There are rows of beautifully groomed oak trees. Lilly would love to roll on the ground, which was a combination of dirt and fine pebbles—she'd be a mess afterward! Sometimes we'd take the bus [dogs welcome, of course] to Jardin du Luxembourg. The palace and grounds were initially developed by Marie de Médicis, who married Henry IV; now it houses the French Senate. There are stunning fountains here, and so many dogs."

Some dog-oriented services—like dog sitting and professional dog walkers—are less a part of Parisian canine culture. But in this international center of style and couture, grooming is de rigueur. "Lilly is a miniature goldendoodle and needs pretty regular grooming," Carolyn said. "When we picked her up from her first grooming in Paris, the stylists had given her the quintessential poodle look—shaved legs, dome head, puffed-out tail. My first response was, 'What dog is this?' When I caught my breath, I assured the groomer that this style was very nice, but Lilly would prefer a less formal styling next time."

Many Americans will often look longingly at the Parisian lifestyle—shorter work-weeks, longer vacations, more leisurely meals. Parisians know how to *live*. Carolyn was left with that feeling while on a brief sojourn back in America. "We had retained a dog sitter in Paris to help with Lilly when we had to travel for work or our children's sports. She did a wonderful job. We were slated to visit our family back in New Jersey one summer, and decided that Lilly would stay in France. The dog sitter offered to take Lilly into her own home for the summer. We were staying in a sweltering beach house on the Jersey Shore with no breeze and no air-conditioning. One day, the dog sitter sent a picture of Lilly sitting by an infinity pool, with the coastline of Biarritz in the background. We were left thinking, 'How can it be that we're in a hot crowded beach house while our dog is poolside in elegant Biarritz'!"

CAROLYN RYAN HEALEY operates a foundation focused on education and environmental and water conservation causes, and also works as a life coach and executive coach. She loves tennis, paddleball and pickleball, golf, long beach walks, and travel. Since returning to the US from Paris with her husband, daughters, and dog, Lilly, Carolyn has called Princeton, New Jersey, home.

If You Go

▶ **Getting There:** Charles de Gaulle Airport is served by most major carriers, including Air France (airfrance.com).
▶ **Best Time to Visit:** Paris has its charms throughout the year; many Parisians leave the city in the summer, which may make for less-crowded cafés . . . but also less interaction with local folks.
▶ **Accommodations:** Paris boasts more than eight hundred dog-friendly hotels. Bonjour Paris (bonjourparis.com) and the Paris Convention and Visitors Bureau (en.parisinfo .com) list a range of options.
▶ **Supplies:** Paris offers many stores for your dog, including Two Tails (www.twotails.fr) and Dog in the City (+33 42740711; www.doginthecity.fr).

ATLANTA

RECOMMENDED BY **Julie Chabot**

"When I first moved to Atlanta, I didn't realize how big the dog community was," Julie Chabot began. "I knew I wanted to get a dog. I adopted Glenn, my hound rescue dog, from Furkids Atlanta and was so excited to explore Atlanta with him, but I wasn't expecting the culture to be so pet-friendly. The younger generation tends to treat their dogs like their children. Atlanta seems to get that. There are so many dog-friendly events. There are hikes, meetups at breweries, walks on the BeltLine. People get together in groups and visit all the dog-friendly patios together. It's very easy to get into the dog community here."

Georgia's capital city is famous for its grits—both breakfast and political. The unofficial cultural capital of the South, Atlanta was the birthplace of Coca-Cola in the 1930s, the cradle of the civil rights movement in the 1960s, and the stomping grounds of some of the most genre-defining hip-hop artists in the 1980s and '90s. Long, balmy summers and brief winters allow "Hotlanta's" incredible greenery to bloom year-round, and outdoor spaces (and culture) flourish with life.

Today the city's downtown is connected through the BeltLine, a twenty-two-mile network of former railroad tracks transformed to link neighborhoods together. "One of my favorite things to do with Glenn was to take him on the BeltLine," described Julie. "Tons of people take their dogs here, and for good reason. It is not just any old bike path. They have group runs, murals, trees, cafés, street art projects. This woman went around hiding tiny little doors everywhere along the path, and Glenn and I used to go out and find them.

"An interesting thing about Atlanta is that you are in a city, but then you take one step away and you're suddenly just surrounded by trees. Hiking with your dog is big out here, and the first trail that comes to mind is called Cochran Shoals, which is just north of

OPPOSITE:
Dog-friendly
beer gardens and
outdoor patios
decorate Atlanta's
cityscape.

DESTINATION 22

Atlanta proper. It's very flat, like a walking path, but it's completely surrounded by greenery. The Chattahoochee River runs right along it. A bit south of that is the Indian Trail in the East Palisades area, which weaves in and out of bamboo forests, the kind you have to crane your neck up to see the top of. A bit further north from the East Palisades area, there's Vickery Creek. It's a beautiful five-mile trail to this spectacular waterfall. Not the sort of thing you'd expect to be so close to a major city."

Closer to downtown, visitors can check out Morningside Nature Preserve. Carefully protected by neighborhood residents and the Nature Conservancy, it serves as an inner-city woodland retreat in the midst of Atlanta's midtown. Walk through the wooded glades and over the suspension bridge, and you'll be at Atlanta's most popular dog beach along the shores of Peachtree Creek. "There's tons of little pockets of greenery like this throughout the city," Julie observed. "Morningside Nature Preserve is a wonderful place to take your dog in summer."

To beat the heat that presses on through autumn, discerning pups might consider a stop at Piedmont Park. The city's largest green space hosts an annual Splish Splash Doggie Bash, where the park's community pools open their doors for dogs in need of a cool swim. All funds raised go on to fund the Piedmont dog parks. "It's a great park to take your dog in general," Julie said. "They have two enclosed off-leash areas, one dedicated to big breeds and one for small. There's also a huge patio restaurant there, with something like fifty tables, and it's super dog-friendly."

"Halcyon is another neighborhood where everything is dog-friendly. You can take your dog into the shops, the restaurants. They have a Santa Paws at Christmas, and Yappy Hours. There is even a trail that runs through the Halcyon called Big Creek Greenway. I think it was recently named the most dog-friendly development by *Atlanta* magazine."

The restaurant scene boasts breweries with dog-friendly beer gardens and patios where groups can while away long summer evenings over whiskey and wine. A particular place of note is Fetch, designed for almost every occasion you could possibly want to attend with your dog. "Essentially it's a dog park bar," Julie explained. "They have a location in Old Fourth Ward, and another in Buckhead. The properties are over twenty thousand square feet, and there are cooling stations and shaded areas for dogs. There's also a full-service bar inside of an Airstream. They host comedy shows, holiday parties and movie nights in the park. They even have Wi-Fi, so it's a great place to come and cowork. 'Bark rangers' go around and make sure all the dogs are playing nicely together."

DESTINATION 22

Another popular weekend pastime in autumn is a winery visit with your pup. A one- to two-hour car ride takes visitors to the outskirts of the city, where trees are bursting with the sunset palette of fall. Small, family-run vineyards and grand commercial tasting rooms alike typically welcome dogs on patios. Be sure to sample the muscadine grape and various fruit wines (think blackberry and, of course, peach), which are local specialties.

"I thought I was going to be in Atlanta for a few years and then go back to Florida," Julie concluded. "But it's such a great place to live. It's the perfect mix of city as well as nature. There's a little bit of something for everyone. I feel like you can take your dog just about everywhere."

JULIE CHABOT coins herself a "crazy dog mom" and loves adventuring with her chocolate Lab rescue, Ernie. As a learning and development specialist by day and Instagram content creator by night, Julie loves sharing Ernie's experiences and personality with the Instagram community. You can follow Ernie at @Ernie_thepupper. Though she recently moved to Orlando, Florida, after spending seven years in Atlanta, Georgia, she believes Atlanta is the most dog-friendly city in America! Never fear, for she, her fiancé, Sammy, and Ernie will still have the ability to travel to Atlanta frequently to visit family. Her love for dogs began when she adopted Glenn, her hound rescue dog, from Furkids Animal Shelter and Rescue; he passed away at the age of three due to epilepsy. She still misses him every day, but feels him with her in every adventure she shares with Ernie.

If You Go

► **Getting There:** Atlanta is served by most major carriers and is a hub for Delta (800-221-1212; delta.com).
► **Best Time to Visit:** Autumn is a great time to visit wineries and see the changing colors. Summers can be quite humid.
► **Accommodations:** A list of reliable dog-friendly hotels can be found at visitatlanta.com.
► **Supplies:** Atlanta has several pet stores, but a consistent favorite is the Whole Dog Market (404-549-2727; thewholedogmarket.com).

DESTINATION 22

CHICAGO

RECOMMENDED BY **Lindsey Tom**

Chicago is all about dogs—whether it's enjoying the famous poppy-seed-bun hot dog, or cheering from the stands of Impact Field, the Chicago Dogs' baseball stadium. It's also a great place to take your dog on a stroll, whether through the city's incredible array of historical skyscrapers, or into a green forest preserve in the city's outer limits. "Chicago is a pretty dog-friendly city," began Lindsey Tom. "It has a really large park system within the city, and a large forest preserve network out in the suburbs. It wasn't until we got Orion that we realized how many green spaces there were, and how many trails there were within the forest preserve system. I feel very fortunate to live in a city that has so many."

Chicago's robust network of DFAs (dog-friendly areas) is kept up to date on the Chicago Parks District website. Within the downtown area, some favorites include Ping Tom Memorial Park, which also happens to be inside the city's famous Chinatown. Here, seventeen acres of rolling green meadows and expansive river views welcome both humans and dogs alike for a quick break from Chicago's hustle and bustle. "Memorial Park has wonderful views of the city," continued Lindsey. "You can pick up some great dim sum while you're there, too. We particularly like MingHin."

No trip to Chicago would be complete without a walk along the shores of Lake Michigan. Beaches and paved sidewalks line most of the shoreline; one favorite is Montrose Beach, a 3.83-acre dog-friendly park near the north end of the city. On a hot day, the blond sandy beach might make you do a double take to ensure you aren't in Southern California, and the bright blue waters of Lake Michigan make for wonderful paw refreshment.

"One particularly cool dog park is Jackson Bark," continued Lindsey. "It's an indoor/outdoor space across from Jackson Park on the South Side. I think it wins best dog park

OPPOSITE:
Chicago has
miles of dog-
friendly parks
and beaches,
including the
shoreline of
Lake Michigan.

DESTINATION 23

of Chicago just about every year. It's a makeshift agility course, built with street signs, tires, refurbished construction gear, and other things like that. It's a big playground for dogs, basically. They have so much fun. And it's free. Because it's community run, everyone is respectful of keeping it clean; there's hardly any trash. Jackson Park, which surrounds the Bark, is its own large and lovely park, with museums and fountains among other attractions. It's spacious, and because it's a little further out from downtown, it's not as crowded as some other parks. In the spring it's the best spot to check out cherry blossoms, and it's also close to the lakefront, so if you want to leave the park and walk along the lake, you can easily find a path that connects up."

If you want even more space, Beck Lake, Bremen Grove, and Miller Meadow are three wonderful forest preserve parks just outside the city that allow dogs to roam off-leash. A network of trails connects the parks together, allowing dog walkers to create their own unique hikes.

Chicago has balmy summers that make for perfect hiking and beach days, but the winters are notoriously snowy. Still, for some dogs, this is the happiest time of year. "The most memorable moment we had with Orion was our first winter with him," Lindsey recalled. "It was January 2021, and we got a massive amount of snow. It was his first time seeing the snow. The drifts were over our waists, and one morning we woke up early to walk him, and the snowplows hadn't come through yet. So he ended up just swimming through the snow in the park. He literally paved his own path right through the snow. It was so cold; I was miserable, with snow in my boots. But he was having the time of his life, so proud of the little path he paved."

After a day of park exploration, Chicago's foodie scene awaits. The city's famous hot dog carts are dog-friendly by design, and there's a robust scene of breweries and patios that's not to be missed. "A lot of restaurants have their own doggy menus," continued Lindsey. "A favorite of ours is Bar Siena, which has a spacious front patio, and also the Perch. It's a little quieter, there's lots of shade, and the staff is just so amazing. They always make sure everyone is comfortable and has everything they need."

Chicago has a burgeoning craft beer scene, and breweries are dog-friendly almost as a rule. A particular favorite is Midwest Coast Brewery. "It's a little bit further west from downtown, but worth the trip," Lindsey noted. "They have a big patio, and dogs are allowed inside. They partner with the local community, and there's often lots of local food pop-ups. It's just a wonderful scene.

"Chicago has tons of dog-friendly restaurants, bars, shops, and there really is something for everyone," Lindsey concluded. "My recommendation to anyone coming here is to think about what kind of experience you want—more urban, more nature-based, more upscale—and then choose what you want to do based off of that. I love doing the river walk with Orion, but there's lots of people on those inner-city trails. If you want more isolation, you can hike in the parks of forest preserves, and go to a brewery after. Chicago has enough of everything to cover a lot of experiences. You can always find whatever works best for you and your dog."

LINDSEY TOM is the proud Chinese American dog mom of Orion, a red Shiba Inu. You can find her on Instagram at @OrionInTheChi, sharing adventures and scenes from her travels around Chicago and beyond with Orion and her husband. While she enjoys taking beautiful photos of Orion, she also shares her raw and funny moments with him, because life with dogs is more than just pretty pictures. Lindsey's Instagram account for Orion is an LGBTQIA+ and BIPOC-safe space and she enjoys connecting on social media with like-minded dog owners who also care about social justice, creating accessible and inclusive content, training the dog in front of them, and supporting their local communities through mutual aid programs and funds.

If You Go

▶ **Getting There:** Chicago is served by two major aiports: O'Hare, a hub for both United (800-864-8331; united.com) and American (800-433-7300; aa.com), and Midway, a hub for Southwest (800-435-9792; southwest.com).

▶ **Best Time to Visit:** If your dog loves the snow, Chicago's winters will be welcoming. Spring and summer tend to have the best lake and hiking weather.

▶ **Accommodations:** Choose Chicago lists several hotels that welcome dogs at choose chicago.com

▶ **Supplies:** Chicago has a large number of pet shops. If you're downtown, check out Tails in the City (800-266-1118; tailsinthecity.com) for luxurious goodies and upscale treats.

VENICE

RECOMMENDED BY **Shandos Cleaver**

"For me, the attraction of Venice isn't the famous buildings and squares, although they are certainly not to be missed," Shandos Cleaver began. "It's about exploring this strange city built upon a lagoon. It's one of those places where you can choose a rough direction to head, and then suddenly you're alone, out of the crowds, wandering down alleyways and past canals, admiring the facades of elaborate palaces and churches, the many bridges and fountains . . . You'll never know what you'll find. It's just the perfect thing to do with a dog by your side—perhaps they might also stop you from so easily getting lost!"

Visitors flock to Italy's watery, UNESCO World Heritage city to take in its renaissance palaces, byzantine mosaics, and famed gondola rides. A lesser-known fact is that Fido is welcome on the boat, too. This is one facet of a broader dog-friendly attitude, integral to Italian culture that is exemplified in Venice especially. "When I first came, we did a bit of a road trip around northern Italy and then took the train over to Venice," reflected Shandos. "One aspect I quickly noticed about Italian culture is that it is quite dog-friendly, particularly in the north. This is partially due to regulations that allow dogs to visit many places. But also, Italians tend to have a relaxed attitude toward what rules do exist, and perhaps bend them."

In Venice, the famous cobblestone walkways between Rialto Bridge and Piazza San Marco are must-do items on any tourist's bucket list, where throngs of visitors can appreciate the gilded domes of Saint Mark's Basilica and stare in awe at the towering figure of the campanile. "One of our miniature dachshund Schnitzel's favorite things was to visit Saint Mark's Square, down near the waterfront, between the basilica and the palace," Shandos continued. "If you go earlier in the morning, you can beat the crowds. It's calmer, more serene, and there are usually huge flocks of pigeons. Schnitzel used to love

OPPOSITE:

A little-known fact about Venice is that dogs are typically welcome on gondola rides.

24

DESTINATION

to dive into them, and they would scatter everywhere, like a pile of leaves that keeps filling up. The pigeons aren't afraid, and he never hurt them, but it was fun to watch these two parts of nature interact in this very gilded area."

Venice in the summer can get crowded, especially around the main tourist sites. For a break, consider heading off into the alleys of the San Marco district, in between the Grand Canal and Piazza San Marco, or venture into the northern Cannaregio district, which includes historical memorials from its time serving as the city's Jewish ghetto (these days, the quiet neighborhood district is home to many of Venice's full-time residents).

Visitors can also consider checking out one of the many small islands that frame Venice, most of which are just a short boat ride away. "You can take a vaporetto, which is like a waterbus; a form of public transport that goes between the islands," continued Shandos. "We went to an island called Burano, which is famous for its colorful houses. It's a beautiful spot to go, very photogenic. It's part of Venice, but the atmosphere is completely different. Fewer crowds, more open air rather than little alleyways, and a lot more green grass.

"Because we had a dog, people would sometimes assume we were locals. Tourists would stop us and ask us for directions. My Italian was terrible, but just having the dog, I noticed people treated me differently, more like I belonged."

Like the water-based transit options, most restaurants in Venice are dog-friendly. Patios and terraces allow visitors to sit and enjoy a Spritz Veneziano or a Bellini (both born in the city) and savor the lights of the city sparking to life. While it's always good to have a few places in mind before you head out into the night, don't be surprised if you get turned around in the atmospheric maze of laneways. "Trying to find somewhere in Venice for the second time is always a challenge," Shandos said. "There was this wonderful wine bar and restaurant we visited, and I could not locate it for the longest time. My husband was finally able to find it, years later—it's called Cantina Do Spade. When we visited, I'm pretty sure it was so crowded, we sat outside in the alleyway, but they allow dogs inside as well. They're particularly renowned for their cicchetti and appetizers, which are like Venetian tapas."

Venice offers many pet-friendly hotels and privately rented apartments. You and your pet can enjoy the rococo opulence of Hotel Danieli, or save your dollars for the gondola and escape to the more budget-friendly Hotel Abbazia or Hotel Ca' dei Conti, just a few of the many hotels that do not charge a pet fee.

"We stayed right along the grand canal, in an apartment, which was not too hard to find," Shandos concluded. "Some apartments have small grassy lawns, where your pet can have a better time relieving themselves. And also, in the evening, which is my favorite time, you can step outside and watch a quiet version of Venice appear. The day-trippers have left the city, a stillness descends, and you can slowly watch all the lights come on in the facades, reflecting over the water. It's magical."

SHANDOS CLEAVER is the founder of *Travelnuity* (travelnuity.com), the top-ranking dog-friendly travel blog in Australia and Europe, focused on dog-friendly travel around the world. She's passionate about providing inspiration and information to others wanting to travel with their dogs, whether close to home or internationally. When not traveling around the world, Shandos lives in Sydney, Australia, along with her husband and their miniature dachshund, Schnitzel. Together they've traveled extensively throughout Australia, the United States, and Europe, with Schnitzel so far ticking off an impressive thirty-six countries. Shandos and Schnitzel have been interviewed together on BBC World News, profiled by ABC (Australia), and provided tips to *New York* magazine, *Escape* (Australia), and *Baltic Outlook* inflight magazine.

24

DESTINATION

If You Go

▶ **Getting There:** Marco Polo airport in Venice is served by Delta (800-221-1212; delta.com), American Airlines (800-433-7300; aa.com), and Alitalia (800-223-5730; alitalia.com) that fly routes from a small handful of eastern US cities during peak season. Some travelers find it easier to fly into Milan's Malpensa Airport, then catch a train to the Santa Lucia station on the northwestern edge of Venice.

▶ **Best Time to Visit:** Summer is the peak tourist season and the best weather. Fall offers slightly diminished crowds paired with colder temperatures.

▶ **Accommodations:** The Venice Tourism Board has a list of reliable flats to rent at visit-venice-italy.com/holiday-flats-venice-italy.htm.

▶ **Supplies:** There are a select handful of pet supply shops in Venice, including Celeste Pet Shop (+39 041 522 8889; www.celestevenezia.it).

KOYARU

RECOMMENDED BY **Kimiko Takemura**

"I first came to Doggy's Island in 2015," began Kimiko Takemura. "I brought Gustav, my miniature dachshund, along with me, for a public relations event I was working on. I liked it so much, I kept coming back. Now I can't count how many times I've returned."

As of 2021, Japan reported a total of 8.9 million dogs and 9.5 million cats, making it the only country in the world where pets outnumber children. Tokyo has cultivated a thriving culture around pet pampering, and in upscale neighborhoods, canine spas are as common (and as glamorous) as those that cater to humans. Dog acupuncture and aroma-therapy are increasingly common treatments, and the expert manicurists at posh salons such as Joke, I am Candy, or Bubble allow you and your best friend to leave with matching claws. Tourists can attempt to snag an appointment with master dog groomers Yoriko Hamachiyo, famous for his rounded, full body shapes, or Shigetomo Egashira (better known as the DogMan) to help find your dog's natural, custom-tailored look. After a day of pampering, both dog and human can enjoy authentic izakaya tableside at Orenchi, or opt for a tray of chef-selected meats and vegetables at Yasaiya Teppanyaki Yasai (if you call ahead, you can reserve a birthday plate for your pup).

But aside from these known havens of luxury, Tokyo is not broadly known for its dog-friendliness. Most places do not allow dogs inside. Only small dogs in carriers are allowed on public transportation. You can get around with Pet Taxi Smile, a fleet of brightly colored Volkswagen buses that will carry you wherever you and your dog need to go in the city. But often it can be a game of trying to figure out where you'll be welcome or, most often, not. "I always try to take Gustav with me when I go out," reflected Kimiko. "But in Japan, it can be difficult to bring dogs to, say, a normal restaurant. It's not like in France, or Italy. Still, I try to take him with me, because he's quiet and polite. However, even if

OPPOSITE:
Dogs are treated like royalty in Japan's resort town of Koyaru.

your dog is well trained, you still often feel you are not welcome. But at Doggy's Island, everything is completely different. It's like he can be a dog, he can be free."

About sixty kilometers east of Tokyo, in the prefecture of Chiba, lies Doggy's Island (not to be confused with Inujima, aka "Dog Island," off the coast of Okayama). Doggy's Island is a hotel that is a destination unto itself, a resort dedicated equally to (if not more so than) the comfort and health of its canine guests and its human ones. "It's kind of in the middle of nowhere," chuckled Kimiko. "I grew up in Tokyo, and Chiba always struck me as the countryside, even though you are only an hour outside the city. But as you approach Doggy's Island, the city fades away. There are all these lovely trees, the air gets very fresh. You're suddenly in nature."

Doggy's Island began as a simple hotel on the town of Koyaru, where humans and dogs could enjoy a vacation together. As time has gone on, the hotel now resembles its own village, complete with nature walks, a pizzeria and bakery, multiple parks, canine swimming pools, and a traditional *onsen* spa for humans.

The result is an experience for dogs that is "like a kindergarten," according to Kimiko. "Some people bring one dog. Some people bring eight. Dogs are everywhere, playing with each other, roaming free in all the space, being very happy." Above and beyond your average pet-friendly hotel, each room comes standard with toilet sheets, toilet trays, poop bags, tableware, dog towels, cushions, adhesive cleaners, deodorants, lanterns, and walking bags. Outside the hotel room, when considering what you can do with your pup, it's easier to count the areas where dogs *aren't* allowed (the onsen and your hotel room's Jacuzzi tub), since the culture is built to treat them as a welcome guest. Just about every activity is designed to be shared between humans and pups. Each mealtime includes a chef's handmade dog menu, and the grounds feature multiple swimming pools and splash ponds, some reserved for small breeds, others welcoming bigger dogs. The Forest Walk area allows for some leisurely forest bathing, and a 1.7-acre dog run (the largest grass dog park in Japan) sits at the ready, complete with misters to combat heat and an awning to protect against any sudden summer rainstorms.

"The nice thing is, it's only an hour from Tokyo," reflected Kimiko. "So if you are in Tokyo but want to take your dog to a place where you both can get away, you can just drive over, maybe have lunch or dinner, let your dog run in the beautiful park. You can relax, your dog can play with other dogs, and then you can head back to Tokyo whenever you need to."

DESTINATION

25

The hotel does offer a kenneling service if you want to visit the rest of the sites in the little village of Koyaru. "There's a golf course next door to the hotel," explained Kimiko, "and also a fasting hotel. This is kind of a boom in Japan right now for health-conscious people. You can check in more than a night (two nights or more). They keep track of your health, your nutrition, giving you cold pressed juices, supplements, detox teas. And there are some other activities like yoga and meditation. It's a lovely way to relax. All of this is right next door to Doggy's Island.

"When we're traveling with dogs, we always have to think, 'Oh, can I do this? Can I do that? Will be he okay, will other people be okay if he's with me?' But at Doggy's Island, it's the opposite. You don't have to worry. There are no problems. You can just go. The staff are wonderful and help take care of the dogs. Sometimes I go there to relax, or to work on my laptop, while Gustav can play with the dog friends he has made there. It's a perfect getaway for both of you, human and dog."

KIMIKO TAKEMURA started her career in PR and consulting in the health and beauty field and has expanded to various high-end fields such as alcohol, luxury watches, celebrity chefs, restaurants, bars, cruise trips, skincare, and so on. She has over twenty years of professional PR experience, and her agency, Gustav Communications (which she named after her beloved dog, Gustav), is celebrating its tenth anniversary in 2022. On the side, Kimiko works with a community group that helps rescue neglected pets.

If You Go

▶ **Getting There:** Both of Tokyo's international airports (Narita and Haneda) are hubs for Japan Airlines (800-525-3663; jal.com). Narita is in Chiba, closer to Koyaru.
▶ **Best Time to Visit:** Spring is a coveted season to watch the blooms of plum and cherry trees. Autumn sees lower crowds and fewer rainy days than the summer months.
▶ **Accommodations:** Doggy's Island Resort & Villa (+81 43-312-1110; doggys-island.jp/en) takes bookings year-round and will have all the supplies your dog could possibly need.

MOUNT DESERT ISLAND

RECOMMENDED BY **Kim Swan**

"Many people that come to the Bar Harbor and Acadia area are outdoorsy sorts," Kim Swan began. "And outdoors people are often dog people." Odds are good that neither visiting dogs nor their owners will be disappointed when they arrive at the hub of "Down East" Maine.

Both the town of Bar Harbor and Acadia National Park sit on Mount Desert Island, a collection of granite headlands, rocky beaches, and spruce-fir forests approximately three-quarters of the way up Maine's sprawling coastline, and an hour or so's drive southeast from the city of Bangor. (Mount Desert Island is also the second-largest island on the Eastern Seaboard of the US; Long Island in New York is the largest.) The stunning beauty of the region began attracting "gilded age" families from Philadelphia, New York, and Boston to the region in the latter part of the nineteenth century, drawn at least in part by the work of painters from the Hudson River School, including Frederic Church and Thomas Cole. The affluent of the Gay Nineties (including the Rockefellers, Vanderbilts, and Carnegies) built grand estates on the island, to which they decamped for a portion of each summer.

While the so-called robber barons changed the social face of Mount Desert Island, they were instrumental in setting aside the land that would eventually become a national park in 1919. Fearing the onslaught the surrounding woodlands would face with the development of a mobile gasoline-powered sawmill, the summer citizenry was galvanized under the leadership of Charles W. Eliot and George B. Dorr, who spearheaded preservation efforts. Dorr would become the park's first superintendent. (John D. Rockefeller contributed another signature facet of the park: its forty-five miles of broken-stone carriage roads, now popular with bicyclists.)

OPPOSITE:
Dogs are welcome in Maine's Acadia National Park, as long as their owners respect the BARK rules (see page 122).

DESTINATION

26

"The chance to visit Acadia National Park is the main draw for visitors to Mount Desert Island, and unlike many national parks, Acadia is dog-friendly," Kim continued. "There are places in the park that are not open to dogs—some of the steeper, scarier trails, for example, and the beaches during the summer season. But dog owners who obey the rules can explore much of the park." Some hundred miles of hiking trails and forty-five miles of carriage roads are open to dogs. Park administrators ask visitors with dogs to join Acadia's Bark Ranger program, which promotes the following behavior:

B = Bag your poop.

A = Always wear a leash.

R = Respect wildlife (especially nesting sites).

K = Know where to go (that is, the trails/carriage roads and other areas open to dogs).

"I love to take my dogs on the carriage roads around Seal Harbor and Jordan Pond," Kim said. "The Jesup Path is definitely a favorite. It's all on a boardwalk that twists and turns through the woods; it's easy on my dogs' feet! In the fall, it's a blanket of red leaves. The Ocean Path trail along Ocean Drive is just gorgeous, showcasing some of the area's most spectacular scenery. By midday it can get a little busy; but early mornings, it's as if you're walking in a painting. It's a spectacular place to watch the sunrise." Looming above the Ocean Path trail is Cadillac Mountain, at 1,530 feet the tallest point along the eastern coast of the United States, offering 360-degree views of Bar Harbor, Frenchman Bay, and the Cranberry Isles. At certain times of year, visitors can hike (or drive) to the summit of Cadillac Mountain to be among the first people in the United States to see the sun. The South Ridge trail is open to dogs, should you wish to walk your dog to the top. "I also love to take the dogs to Little Long Pond," Kim added, "a nature preserve that's just outside the park boundaries, where dogs are allowed off-leash. It's a glorious spot, very popular with dog-loving locals."

When you return to Bar Harbor, there are any number of cafés, pubs, and restaurants awaiting you. "In Bar Harbor, you don't need to leave your dog in the room," Kim explained. "So many restaurants welcome dogs, even the nicer restaurants. A few I enjoy are Paddy's Irish Pub, which is right down on the pier. There are always dogs under the tables there. Havana is one of my favorites; they have a great outdoor space.

Looking Glass has a great deck that welcomes dogs, with an excellent view of the water. The same is true of Stewman's Lobster Pound. If you want to grab a beverage before or after dinner, there's the deck at the Rusticator Lounge at the dog-friendly Bayview Hotel, and the Terrace Grille at the Bar Harbor Inn, a huge hotel that's right downtown. There's a big firepit, and the outside tables all have yellow umbrellas—locals just call it 'Yellow Umbrellas.'"

For many visitors to Down East Maine, the trip is not complete without an opportunity to tie on a bib and tuck into a fresh lobster. In 2021 (the most recent year for which statistics were available as of this writing), over 108 million pounds of lobster were harvested from Maine waters, with many of these succulent crustaceans coming from the cold, nutrient-rich waters off Mount Desert Island. On the plate, *Homarus americanus* can take infinite forms, but in these parts, locals prefer it simple—that is, steamed in shell and served with melted butter and lemon alongside. Most eateries in Bar Harbor feature lobster, but a favorite stop is Jordan Pond House in Acadia. "There's a big lawn in front of the house rolling down to the pond, and people can eat outside at picnic tables," Kim described. "Dogs can lay out on the grass while you have lobster and popovers, which are another Jordan Pond specialty."

KIM SWAN is the owner of Swan Agency Real Estate, where she focuses on business development and selective brokerage of luxury and commercial properties. She also oversees the agency's marketing, public relations, and social media programs. For the past three seasons, she has produced *Living Acadia TV*, a show celebrating the Acadia lifestyle and exploring the coast of Maine, for Fox 22 and ABC7. Kim is dedicated to her community and works with several animal rescue organizations; she is currently on the board of the Bar Harbor Historical Society. She also served ten successful years as a Bar Harbor town councillor. Kim was awarded the 2017 Cadillac Award by the Bar Harbor Chamber of Commerce. She has many business interests throughout Maine, focusing on lodging and real estate investment as well as art, interior design and music publishing. Her most important job, however, is being mom to her darling Yorkies, Ava and Izzi.

DESTINATION

26

If You Go

▶ **Getting There:** Bar Harbor and Acadia National Park are approximately 150 miles north of Portland, Maine, which is served by many major carriers. It's about fifty miles from Bangor, which is served by American Airlines (800-433-7300; aa.com) and Delta (800-221-1212; delta.com).

▶ **Best Time to Visit:** July and August are major tourist times on Mount Desert Island and offer fairly consistent weather. June and September can also be excellent times to visit. The park is open year-round, though beaches are closed to dogs during the summer.

▶ **Accommodations:** There are many dog-friendly lodging options in Bar Harbor, including the Bayview Hotel (207-288-5861; thebayviewbarharbor.com). You'll find more listings at bringfido.com.

▶ **Supplies:** Visit Bark Harbor (207-288-0404; barkharbor.com), conveniently located in downtown Bar Harbor.

DESTINATION

26

PORTLAND

RECOMMENDED BY **Rauni Kew**

Portland—the picturesque and diminutive city (population around 70,000) that rests two hours north of Boston along Maine's Casco Bay—is regularly recognized as one of America's most desirable locales. An extensive urban trails network, a thriving restaurant and beer scene and out-your-front-door access to tranquil bays and beaches attract active-minded visitors from far and wide.

These same qualities make Portland an ideal doggy destination. "Portland is very dog-welcoming," Rauni Kew began. "We have wonderful restaurants, and many started setting up tables for outside dining on the sidewalk and streets during the COVID-19 pandemic. The city has allowed them to remain, so you can eat some fine fare with your dog. Between Portland, South Portland, and Cape Elizabeth, there are many wonderful dog-friendly trails. During the summer, most beaches are closed to dogs from nine to five, and state park beaches are closed to dogs during nesting season. But many beaches in the Portland region have special summer hours when dogs are welcome. In the fall and winter, many beaches are open to dogs all day. Check signs or websites for dog hours, as the hours change. State beaches, in particular, close to dogs in the spring to protect endangered New England cottontail bunnies and piping plovers, a small seabird that nests on the edge of the dunes."

Portland's warm embrace of canines may be best exemplified by Inn by the Sea, a boutique hotel in Cape Elizabeth, overlooking Crescent Beach and in the shadow of one of Maine's most iconic lighthouses, Portland Head Light. "Inn by the Sea began welcoming dogs to stay—at no extra charge—in 1997," Rauni continued. "The owner is very committed to dogs, and wants them to feel as pampered as human guests." This commitment begins with the inn's foster dog program. Inn by the Sea fosters shelter dogs from

the Animal Refuge League of Greater Portland, providing them with a temporary home . . . and the opportunity for guests to walk, play with, and love them. "Inn by the Sea was the first hotel to have rescue dogs on property," Rauni said. "It was a way to bring the Animal Refuge League into the conversation. We have a new dog every few weeks; they stay until they're adopted." As of this writing, 156 dogs have been adopted since the program's launch in 2017.

OPPOSITE: *Visitors to Portland can enjoy many ocean views, like this one near Portland Headlight.*

Dogs visiting the inn with their humans receive water bowls, beach towels, cozy L.L.Bean dog blankets, and handmade treats at turndown. Gourmet pet menus are available for in-room dining or dining on the seaside deck or in the Sea Glass fireplace lounge; offerings include Meat "Roaff" (steamed rice, raw vegetables, natural ground beef), the Bird Dog (grilled chicken, steamed rice, raw vegetables), and K-9 Ice Cream (soy milk honey gelato topped with dog biscuit crumbs). In October, the inn promotes "Going to the Dogs" week, when the pool is closed to humans but open to dogs. "It's just before we close the pool for the winter," Rauni explained, "right after Indigenous Peoples' Day. It's a huge dog pool party. Many of our canine guests will go for a nice walk on the beach, have a swim in the pool, and then adjourn to the lounge for a meal."

To build up your dog's appetite, you might want to see some of the Portland area by foot. Fort Williams Park is the home of the iconic Portland Head Light, and has a number of trails overlooking the ocean within its ninety acres. (The lighthouse dates back to 1791; there's a museum tracing its rich history.) Two of Portland's most popular trails are Back Cove and the Eastern Promenade. Back Cove circles its eponymous body of water (or mud flats at low tide), with great views of Portland's skyline as you look to the east. The Eastern Promenade, which is built along an old narrow-gauge rail corridor, has resplendent views of Portland Harbor and the ocean beyond. During the summer months, there's weekly live music and food carts along the promenade, and the chance to mingle with lots of local dogs.

Touring Portland Head Light and walking the promenade or through the cobblestoned Old Port section of town will certainly give you a sense of Portland. But some time on the water will give you an even better perspective. The Casco Bay Lines ferry is a low-cost, dog-friendly way to get out on the water. "With the ferries, you don't have to plan ahead of time, and dogs are very welcome," Rauni said. "Lots of people will take the ferry out to Peaks Island, which is the first stop. There are trails on the island, and the Inn on

Peaks Island has a big deck where you can grab a drink. If you're enjoying the fresh air, you can stay on the ferry for the whole mail run."

Like so many that visit the Maine coast or call it home, Rauni treasures early evenings spent walking along the beach. "I live right near a fine beach," she concludes, "and I walk my dogs there every day and night. There's always such a joyful cacophony of dogs barking, greeting each other. Experiencing that raises your spirits. Not long ago, I was away, visiting another seaside community. My dogs were home. I went for a walk on the beach. And though it was beautiful, I just didn't enjoy it without my dogs."

RAUNI KEW manages PR and green programs for Inn by the Sea. Previously, she was marketing director for a chemical process manufacturer, launching dispersion equipment that reduced sludge in activated wastewater treatment plants, worked in the technology sector for an Internet screen-sharing provider, and worked in production for CBC television news in New York and at the United Nations. Rauni has served on the Maine Tourism Commission and as chair of the Greater Portland CVB, and is the Greater Portland regional representative for the Maine Office of Tourism Regional Committee. She frequently has published articles on sustainable hospitality in industry journals.

DESTINATION 27

If You Go

▶ **Getting There:** Portland is served by many carriers, including Delta (800-221-1212; delta.com) and United (800-864-8331; united.com).

▶ **Best Time to Visit:** You can count on fairly good weather between mid-May and mid-October.

▶ **Accommodations:** Visit Portland (207-772-5800; visitportland.com) lists a number of dog-friendly lodging options. The Inn by the Sea (207-799-3134; innbythesea.com) gets very high scores from humans . . . and dogs.

▶ **Supplies:** You'll find most of what fido needs one of these stores: Bayside Bark (207-835-0688; baysidebark.com), Loyal Companion (207-797-0779; www.loyalcompanion.com), and Uncommon Paws (888-549-7297; uncommonpaws.com).

BOSTON

RECOMMENDED BY **Liza Ryus**

The city that jump-started America's independence also lets freedom ring for its canine citizens. The number of dog owners grows exponentially every year, and it's easy to see why. Boston Common contains America's first unfenced off-leash dog zone, and Boston is the only city in the country with a dog breed named after it (the Boston terrier, sometimes fondly referred to as "the American Gentleman.")

"When I started my graduate program at Boston University, I came from California with my dog, Pete the Schnauzer," began Liza Ryus. "And we basically came from the sticks. Pete had barely ever been on a leash. I'll never forget him seeing the T [the city's train system] for the first time. We were waiting to walk across the street. And of course, the T is embedded across the sidewalk; there's no separate platform. So, the train approached, and Pete started whining and getting really scared. I realized what was happening, crouched down, and picked him up to comfort him. But that was just the first week. Now he rides the train like a pro. People say hello to him, he makes friends, and everyone is nice to us, because people are used to dogs being on the T."

Boston is a notoriously dog-friendly city, but in a way that reflects the city's unique style: familial and pragmatic, all at once. "Dogs are not pampered here in the way that they are in California," mused Liza. "Dogs are dogs here. At the same time, you love your dog. Your neighbors love their dogs. You take your dog everywhere, and this is considered pretty normal. But your dog is allowed to actually be a dog."

One of the best parts of Boston for both dogs and humans is its walkability. The famous Freedom Trail is an ideal way to catch at least sixteen of the city's most prominent historical sites. Simply follow the redbrick path in the sidewalk from the Boston National Historic Park at the Charleston Navy Yard, past the Paul Revere House and Independence

Hall. A stop at Faneuil Hall's dog-friendly boutiques is a worthy detour (come during Halloween to enter your pup in the costumed pet parade). Next door, the Quincy Market building has numerous dog-friendly restaurants, and famous cider donuts and lobster rolls for the humans. It might not be a true trip to Boston without at least one stop at a Dunkin'—the internationally famous coffee chain was born here. Several franchises dot the trail, and pup cups are a menu standard.

The Freedom Trail ends at Boston Common, America's oldest city park, grand and snowy in the winter, and bursting with green leaves and music in the summer. Nearby, pleasure cruises and whale-watching tours can be chartered on Boston Harbor, and water-loving dogs can hop aboard along with their humans and enjoy the brisk sea air.

"Outside of downtown, some of our dog's favorite parks are Rogers Park and Savin Hill," described Liza. "Rogers Park includes an enclosed baseball diamond, where dogs can run free and make friends. Savin Hill is in Dorchester, at the southern end of the city. You walk up a short stone hill and get a beautiful view along the bay. There's an interesting old fort, and there's always some boats hanging out in the harbor. It's a really nice little escape. You're still in the city, but it feels like it's just you, the ocean, and the trees.

"Every bar and restaurant, even before the pandemic, usually had a patio where you could have your dog. There's a whole bunch of really cool places in Brookline, Somerville, and Cambridge, almost too many to count. A favorite of ours is the Abbey, in Brighton. It's an upscale pub with a beautiful patio. They have dog lollipops, which are little chunks of meat on the bone that the servers will bring out.

"Another great place, a little west from downtown, is Rosebud American Kitchen & Bar. The restaurant is in the shape of a vintage train car. The food is great, the cocktails are great. But if you walk your dog through the lobby of the restaurant, toward the back door, there is this really cute patio. Everyone hangs out there, and in the summer, the waiters always make sure your dog has water."

There are also a few businesses that cater directly to dogs rather than their humans. Polkadog, which has a few locations, offers a gourmet buffet of canine novelties, including "Bad Spaniels" squeaky toys shaped like bottles of whiskey and handmade jerky. If your dog has a birthday or adoption day approaching, consider a stop to Dog Eat Cake, a bakery providing professionally decorated, custom canine cakes.

Within a short drive of downtown Boston, there are preserved slices of nature. To the city's south, Blue Hills Reservation is one of the largest parks in the state, with hundreds of miles of trails, all of which are dog-friendly (keep in mind that leashes are required). During the autumn, the park is an excellent place to view New England's brilliant changing leaves. A brief drive north of the city, Middlesex Fells Reservation offers 2,200 acres of dog-friendly hiking, including Sheep's Meadow, where dogs are allowed to roam off-leash. In the summer, canoe rentals are available on Spot Lake.

"You can have a really good experience being a dog owner here," Liza concluded. "People don't look surprised when you show up with your dog. There's significantly less judgment than I've received in other places, where someone would suggest a dog behaviorist if your dog so much as made a noise outside. But that's in line with the Boston spirit."

LIZA RYUS is the proud mom of rescue dogs Pete the schnauzer and Mica the silver Lab. Originally from Chicago, she spent ten years in Northern California working in the entertainment industry before moving to Massachusetts in 2019. Liza has done crafts, costumes, puppets, and dye work for the San Francisco Opera, *MythBusters*, and Fonco Studios. In February 2020, Liza launched a promising line of home craft kits starring her original cast of characters, the Millenimals, and in 2022 finished her second MFA in theater costuming and craftswork at Boston University. She now operates her own production studio, Brush & Blade, in Pawtucket, Rhode Island, where the Millenimals will make their second commercial debut in fall 2022. Liza lives in Boston, Massachusetts, with her wife and family.

DESTINATION

28

If You Go

▶ **Getting There:** Boston Logan International Airport is served by most major carriers.
▶ **Best Time to Visit:** The winters are famously rough. Consider visiting during the long, green days of summer, or catch the spectacular colors of fall's changing leaves.
▶ **Accommodations:** The Greater Boston Convention & Visitors Bureau (bostonusa .com) lists a number of dog-friendly options.
▶ **Supplies:** Polkadog (polkadog.com) has a few locations across the city.

THE CATSKILLS

RECOMMENDED BY **Janice Costa**

"I wanted to adopt a rescue after my fifteen-year-old dog passed," began Janice Costa. "That's how I got Jessie, my shepherd/Malinois mix. She was so protective, we jokingly called her Cujo; I could barely have anyone in my house. I was out of my league; I had no idea what to do about her behavior. People told me to put her to sleep. But I had already looked her in the eye and said she was safe, and I was going to take care of her. Finally, I found the right trainer to work with us, and as I learned more about her and our bond grew, she was transformed into a wonderful, well-behaved dog. But then when it came time for a vacation, I realized I didn't want to leave her behind. This was in 2009; it was hard to find a place anyone would welcome you with a dog, especially a big dog. Even if they did, most places required that your dog be under twenty pounds. There were no options for people like me.

"So I broke open my funds and started calling hotels, seeing if we could start a little vacation group for dog owners I knew who had a similar problem. They'd ask, 'You want to bring *how* many dogs?' Some just hung up on me. But eventually, I found a place that would give us a chance. That's how Canine Camp Getaway was born."

The Catskill Mountains are a haven for the urban denizens of New York, a green escape from the hustle and bustle of city life with wide-open fields, miles of hiking trails through the countryside, picturesque creeks, and rustic boutique hotels. The Catskills have a dog-friendly reputation: You can stroll the grounds of the Thomas Cole National Historic Site or one of the seasonal farmers' markets, enjoy brunch at Mountain Dog Cafe, or stay the night at the Bavarian Manor Inn, all with Fido at your side. However, there is one particular venue that doesn't just allow dogs, it caters to their very idea of fun.

OPPOSITE: Dogs can compete in agility courses at Canine Camp Getaway, a doggy summer camp in the Catskills.

DESTINATION 29

In East Durham, a small village in the northern Catskills, there's an event each September that allows your dog to feel like they are at their very own summer camp. "I asked myself, 'What would be my dog's dream vacation?'" reflected Janice. "And that's what led our planning."

Canine Camp Getaway is a four-day dog-cation, with a rotating list of activities including flyball, barks and crafts, an animal charity auction, agility and lure coursing, and barn hunts. "In addition to the games, we have a holistic and traditional veterinarian on-site, and also do therapy dog training and testing," added Janice. "One of my favorite areas is probably the pool. It's entirely dedicated for the dogs' use. Most people don't have access to a pool that allows their dogs to come in, so this is really quite special. It's always such a fun scene. You have labs leaping, goldens splashing, collies and shepherds chasing tennis balls. The little dogs have robes and sunglasses and are laying in the sunchairs. You can feel the sheer joy."

Canine Camp Getaway also has a location in Gettysburg, Pennsylvania, which meets in June. But the Catskills serve as a perfect backdrop for the summer camp vibe. "The Blackthorne Resort, where we hold the camp, is very rustic and tied to the nature around us," Janice continued. "We have AC and meals with full waitstaff, but it's much more of that 'going to camp' feeling. We're bordered by a large forest, acres and acres of greenery, a creek to play in, and there are several big fields so the dogs can really get loose for their agility and lure coursing. It's very scenic, with big views of the mountains and loads of hiking trails.

"Something that I've noticed is that once a dog has been here, if they come back, they remember what this place is. They know their room, they know where the activities are, and they remember their friends, too. And then the new dogs come and pick up on that positive energy."

With so many dogs in one place, you might expect chaos to ensue. But there's enough room for every dog to spread out and enjoy what they truly want to enjoy. "We do screen all dogs before they arrive," Janice explained. "An antisocial dog wouldn't fit in well. But there's also so much room to spread out, and with all the great stuff going on, and all the room for breaks . . . it's not as chaotic as you'd think.

"It was the people, actually, that felt like the biggest variable for me. But I noticed, this became a vacation where you could come even if you didn't know a soul, and you would find people to connect with. I noticed the people whose dogs loved to run agility would hang out. And the people whose dogs liked to swim hung out. Everyone was so incredibly nice to each other. Maybe it's just because dog people tend to be really great people. If someone had a training question, or a sick dog, or anything, people would help each other. People have met here and become lifelong friends.

"At home, you don't get a lot of connected time with your dog when you're not distracted. You're usually on the phone, on the computer, petting them while you watch TV. But out here, you're not distracted. And so you're making memories that you really cherish. You only have your dog for ten to fifteen years, and you want to make them good ones."

Such memories are generated naturally at Canine Camp Getaway. "Jessie was my original ambassadog," Janice said. "She was with me when I first founded the camp, and she passed away in 2015. The first year I did camp without her, it felt very strange. The last night of that year, I remember I walked outside and looked up at the sky and sort of said, 'I miss you, Jessie, I wish you were here.' And on the way home the next day, we stopped at a rest stop, and I ran in to get us lunch and grabbed some sodas. Outside, my sister got this look on her face, picked up the soda, and turned it toward me, and it read 'Have a Coke with Jessie.' So I still feel like she's watching over it, every year. Our camp's own guardian angel dog."

JANICE COSTA has been working with dogs for more than twenty years, and has been planning dog vacations professionally for more than a decade. She is certified as both a therapy dog test examiner and an AKC Canine Good Citizen and trick testing evaluator, and is a certified instructor in pet first aid and canine CPR. Her oldest dog, Lexie, who attended her first camp as a puppy, is a two-time dock diving national champion, her middle dog competes in lure coursing, and her pandemic puppy already won her first regional championship in dock diving. Her dog vacation camp, Canine Camp Getaway, has raised more than $50,000 for animal charities since its inception. When she's not planning dog events, Janice works in the home design industry, and has authored two books, *Grand Master Baths* and *Everything and the Kitchen Sink: Remodel Your Kitchen Without Losing Your Mind*. She is currently at work on a dog memoir, *Jessie's Girl*.

If You Go

▶ **Getting There:** Albany, Hartford and New York City airports are all relatively close to the Catskills. Albany is closest to East Durham and the northern Catskills region.

▶ **Best Time to Visit:** Camp is held in September, but the Catskills have appeal in every season: winter sports, spring and summer hikes, and the beautiful changing of the leaves in the fall.

▶ **Accommodations:** Canine Camp Getaway (877-592-2674; caninecampgetaway.com) is held every year; book in advance.

▶ **Supplies:** East Durham is a rural area, and the nearest pet shops, including Love Thy Beast (518-828-0291; lovetheybeast.com), are in Hudson, about thirty minutes away by car.

DESTINATION

29

MARTINBOROUGH

RECOMMENDED BY **Rachel McIndoe**

When Rachel McIndoe is asked the best place someone could travel with their dog in New Zealand, she takes a thoughtful moment before giving her reply. "There are so many holidays you can take here," she reflected. "You can go to the beach, the mountains, the city. Not every area is as dog-friendly as another. But I think Martinborough comes to the top of the list. It's our wine country—extremely charming, provincial, and so dog-friendly."

The Classic New Zealand Wine Trail covers nearly 292 miles of pastoral roadway, starting in the little town of Seddon on the South Island and heading all the way to Napier at the top of the North Island. Many prefer to tackle smaller chunks of the trail at a time in order to soak up the terroir (and, of course, appropriately appreciate the local vintages). "You can walk or bike the wine trail along with your dog," Rachel said. "The path takes you through all the area's most famous wineries. The thing about New Zealand is that not all the cities are especially dog-friendly, but the wineries very much are. They have great outdoor gardens and patios, which is where you want to be anyway. Most places also have a 'winery dog,' usually a border collie or similar breed, that likes to come and say hello."

Several cities and small towns dot the course of the trail, but a key stop is Martinborough, located about an hour east of New Zealand's coastal capital, Wellington. "Martinborough is a charming historical village, tucked into the hills a bit," continued Rachel. "The area is famous for their pinot noir, and they have about twenty boutique wineries just in the town." Martinborough's wineries tend to be small, family-run affairs, and visitors often opt to rent bikes and pedal between them. "It's hard to say, but my favorite may be Palliser Estate. They have been around for many, many years. Their outdoor area has these big, comfy beanbags, and they offer a seasonal menu with lots of local fruits and vegetables. It was started by a couple, and has continued to be passed down through generations of

the family. And the family *loves* dogs. They recently started releasing some vintage wines, and named each of them after one of the family's beloved dogs. These are their most precious wines, quite limited editions." Other especially dog-friendly wineries include Colombo Martinborough, a small, family-run affair with a large wood-paneled patio and winter firepits, and Luna Estate, with its rustic, open-air tasting room and a focus on organic and sustainable wines.

"If you want to stay in Martinborough for a few days," Rachel noted, "I'd recommend the Brackenridge Country Retreat and Spa. Not all hotels in town are pet-friendly, but this one is a win. You're out in the country, in your own little cottage on a grand estate. It's very tranquil." Vacation rental homes are also a popular choice, and most do allow pets.

After a few days of wine sipping, visitors may start to feel like they need to work off a little of the juice. Luckily, you're in New Zealand, and even if you aren't trying to get a hobbit up a volcano, walks of incomparable beauty are never more than a short drive away. "About twenty minutes down the road from Martinborough is the Cape Palliser Lighthouse walk," said Rachel. "It was built in 1897 and is still used today to guide ships through the Cook Strait, which used to be the site of many shipwrecks. The walk along the coast is very scenic, with incredible views out to sea. Dogs have to stay on-leash, as there's a local fur seal colony that needs to be protected. A good time to visit is actually between November and January, when you can see the seals snuggling with their little pups."

If you are looking for something a bit more intense, an hour's drive south from the vineyards of Martinborough will take you to one of New Zealand's most famous landscapes: the Pinnacles Walk (also known by its original Māori name, the Kauaeranga Kauri Trail). A path from the parking area leads you through green brush, up, and eventually out onto an overlook of spectacular, eerie vaulted rock formations, which were featured in *The Lord of the Rings: The Return of the King*. Another path takes you down through the streambeds, where you can weave between the rocky Pinnacles as they tower overhead. "There are three main tracks," Rachel explains. "A nice thing about New Zealand is that at the beginning of most walks, there's very clear signage telling you what to look out for, where each one ends, and any rules around how to handle your dog. At Pinnacles, dogs are allowed off-leash, so it's great fun for both of you. But just be sure they are under voice control. New Zealanders are nice, but if your dog misbehaves, you will definitely get some dirty looks!"

If you aren't ready to return back to the green shire of wine country, a dog-friendly campground at Pinnacles is open to adventurous travelers who want to make the most of

OPPOSITE: "Winery dogs" are a common feature of the grape-growing regions of New Zealand.

DESTINATION

30

139

their time there. "Bookings aren't required, and it doesn't tend to fill up," described Rachel. "So you can come in from Martinborough and hike one day, or you can make an overnight of it. This entire area is perfect for enjoying some of New Zealand's highlights with your dog. It's a lovely place."

RACHEL McINDOE is a cofounder and author at *Dog Friendly New Zealand*, the country's largest blog centered on reviewing and exploring pet-friendly local experiences. She is also pet mom to Millie the miniature pinscher (you can follow her antics on Instagram at @millie_minpin). Millie is a recurring character on the TVNZ reality show *Barkley Manor*, which showcases the delight, devotion and drama of life inside a premium doggy day care at one of New Zealand's most esteemed pet facilities. With *Dog Friendly New Zealand,* Rachel hopes to more easily connect locals and vacationers alike with events, hotels, hikes and other experiences where they and their dogs are welcome.

If You Go

► **Getting There:** The nearest airport is in Wellington, New Zealand's capital, and is served primarily by Air New Zealand (800-262-1234; airnewzealand.com). From there, it's about an hour's drive to Martinborough.

► **Best Time to Visit:** January, near the peak of summer in the Southern Hemisphere, is an ideal time. All wineries are open, seal pup season is in swing, and it's not too hot to walk the Pinnacles.

► **Accommodations:** Brackenridge Country Retreat and Spa (+64 6-306 8115; www.brackenridge.co.nz) takes year-round reservations.

► **Supplies:** Thrive Dog Kitchen in nearby Greytown (+64 21 052 6637; thrivedogkitchen.co.nz) has an array of holistic treats and raw foods.

ASHEVILLE

RECOMMENDED BY **Kim Brophey**

Asheville, North Carolina, calls itself "Dog City USA." The slogan is even trademarked. Kim Brophey explained how this came to be: "Asheville is a popular town for tourists, and dogs are also very popular here. People like to take their dogs with them on their travels. We felt 'Dog City USA' could help Asheville with its pet tourism efforts."

Does Asheville live up to its trademark? Most would say yes.

Asheville is an eclectic small city in the Blue Ridge Mountains of western North Carolina where New Agers, outdoor enthusiasts, musicians, and local food advocates all coexist, under a patina of Southern charm that certainly extends to dogs. There's a progressive, hip vibe here that some might not expect in here southern Appalachia, at the gateway to the Great Smokies and the Blue Ridge Mountains. Thanks to its elevation (2,134 feet above sea level), Asheville avoids the intensive heat one might associate with a Carolina summer. George Vanderbilt (of *the* Vanderbilts) recognized the special qualities of the region, choosing Asheville as the site of Biltmore Estate. (When the 250-room mansion was completed in 1895, it was America's largest private home—and remains so today.) The city's thriving food and brewing scene came a bit after George's time, but represents another powerful draw.

One of Dog City USA's unique canine quirks is its Dog Welcome Center. "It's a hop, skip, and a jump away from the Asheville Visitor Center," Kim said. "The folks there will send people with dogs over. We have goodie bags for dog owners that include a map of the city, suggestions for the best hikes in and near town, and a list of all the dog-friendly dining and shopping spots. Visitors can dialogue with staff about activities/places in town that might appeal to the needs of their particular dog. At the Dog Welcome Center, we also try to help people better understand their dogs' behavior and needs. Most dogs

weren't bred to be pets and live in the relatively sterile environments of a house or apartment. They are biological creatures, and when you take out them out of the environment
and away from the tasks they were bred to perform, they develop what humans often call
'behavioral problems'—when really their needs aren't being met by their humans. It's a
form of zoochosis [a type of psychosis that develops in animals held captive in zoos, as
they can't live as they would in the wild]. People aren't intentionally denying their dogs'
needs; they just don't realize their pets crave outlets for their particular genetic expres-
sions." Kim founded the Dog Door to help dog owners understand and meet those needs.

Good food and drink are one important need for dogs (and their humans). Asheville
certainly has this essential covered. "You and your dog could easily spend several days in
Asheville, brewery and restaurant hopping," Kim said. "There are so many dog-friendly
patios, and there's crazy-good people watching; the streets of Asheville are full of the best
sort of insanity." Since Highland Brewing, the first brewpub in Asheville, opened in
1994, the city's blend of outdoorsy and hippie sensibilities have proven the perfect cru-
cible for craft brewing. Today more than thirty small breweries call the region home,
including the eastern outposts of western craft beer superpowers like Sierra Nevada.
Asheville is regularly recognized as one of America's top beer destinations. It's likewise
recognized for its foodie scene, fueled in part by the efforts of chef/restaurateur Meherwan
Irani, who's received four James Beard Award nominations for Best Chef: Southeast.
"You can easily dine out for a week in Asheville with your dog and never visit the same
restaurant twice," Kim added. "One of my favorites is Mountain Madre, which is higher-
end gourmet Mexican fare. They have a lovely outdoor courtyard. Another place I like is
Bouchon, which features French Quarter cuisine. There's a front patio for people watching, and a European courtyard vibe in the back."

When it comes time to walk off some of the fine food and libations you've enjoyed in
Asheville, there are many options available. "If your dog is comfortable with other people
and other dogs, you might enjoy walking in the city proper," Kim advised. "Nearly all of
the stores allow dogs. There's a lovely city park—Pack Square—that's right in the center
of town. In the summer, there's a water feature with spraying fountains. Kids come to
play and dogs love it as a way to cool off." If your dog wants an off-leash experience in
town, the French Broad River Park has a one-acre fenced-in area, and the Azalea Dog Park
has sections for small and large dogs. (Asheville's tour bus trolleys welcome dogs if you
prefer to tour with your feet up!)

OPPOSITE:
A couple of
paddlers enjoy
a day on one of
the many lakes
around Asheville.

DESTINATION

31

143

Outside town, there are countless options. Thanks to Asheville's Blue Ridge Mountain location, hundreds of hiking trails are within a short drive of town, winding past waterfalls or snaking to summits with staggering views. A morning or afternoon wandering the eight-thousand-acre grounds of the Biltmore Estate comes highly recommended. (Note: The interior of the Biltmore and the trails in nearby Great Smoky Mountains National Park are not open to dogs.) Kim also recommends spending a day exploring the Blue Ridge Parkway. "Bring plenty of snacks and water for you and your dog. Pull off at the lookouts to take in the views and stretch your legs. You can't visit Asheville without doing the parkway. A little further out of town, my family also loves to visit Chimney Rock State Park and Lake Lure, especially in the summer. Visit the Rocky Broad River at Chimney Rock with a long leash—if your dog likes water, they'll be in heaven."

By almost any standards, Dog City USA is awash with dog-friendly attractions, and a new dog park, Dog Island, will be opening in 2024. "Dog Island will have three sections—the Farm, the Maze, and the Hunt," Kim explained. "Here dogs will have a chance to express their bred behaviors, like chasing, hunting, and herding."

KIM BROPHEY, CDBC, CPDT-KA, is an applied ethologist and owner of the Dog Door Behavior Center in downtown Asheville, North Carolina. Kim's twenty-year commitment to Family Dog Mediation has been recognized both nationally and locally. She was named the APDT Outstanding Trainer of the Year in 2009 and Best Dog Trainer of Western North Carolina six years in a row. She has lectured and taught courses on canine behavior, ethology, and welfare at colleges, universities, and conferences. Kim is a member of the International Society for Applied Ethology and the Association of Professional Dog Trainers (APDT), and is a past board member of the International Association of Animal Behavior Consultants and the Asheville Humane Society. Kim's trademarked Dog L.E.G.S. (Learning Environment Genetics Self) model is a groundbreaking new system for dog lovers to truly understand their dogs' behavior like never before, distilling multiple scientific disciplines and established principles into a simple and accessible framework for pet dogs and their people. She is launching a coordinated grassroots movement to facilitate a paradigm shift and market disruption in the pet industry through work, which includes a book, *Meet Your Dog: The Game-Changing Guide to Understanding Your Dog's Behavior*; TED Talk ("The Problem with Treating a Dog Like a Pet"); The Dog Key (canine genetic heritage testing software); the National

Dog L.E.G.S. Association for pet-industry businesses and organizations; the L.E.G.S. Applied Ethology Family Dog Mediation Professional Course; and the establishment of Asheville as the official Dog City USA.

If You Go

▶ **Getting There:** Asheville Regional Airport is served by a number of carriers, including American (800-433-7300; aa.com) and Allegiant (702-505-8888; allegiantair.com).

▶ **Best Time to Visit:** May through October, with fine foliage displays in the fall.

▶ **Accommodations:** There are more than 250 pet-friendly lodging options in Asheville, highlighted at exploreasheville.com and bringfido.com. The Aloft Asheville Downtown (828-232-2838; marriott.com) fosters dogs looking for a home, and have matched nearly one hundred dogs to date.

▶ **Supplies:** Asheville has many options for dog supplies; you can find food, accessories, and treats at Woof Gang Bakery & Grooming (828-650-9950; woofgangasheville.com).

DESTINATION

31

TORONTO

RECOMMENDED BY **Ingrid Castro**

"Toronto dog culture has only grown over the years," began Ingrid Castro. "It seems like everybody bought a dog during COVID, and so the inclusivity is rising and restrictions are going down."

Canada's largest metropolis has a well-earned reputation for being dog-friendly year-round. In the upscale Yorkville neighborhood, visitors can treat themselves to a few evenings at the Hazelton Hotel, where every four-legged guest is offered a plushie, elegant dog bowls, treats, and complimentary waste disposal bags. The staff also provides a map outlining the best dog-walking routes in the neighborhood. However, with a city featuring more than sixty off-leash dog parks, wherever you stay in Toronto, you probably won't have to walk far to find a place to let your dog run free.

"Riverdale Park is just great," reflected Ingrid. "There are two sides, one side of the bridge where people let their dogs run in a baseball diamond area, and the other side has a view of the city, where you can watch the sun set. They have farmers' markets in the spring, and you can take your dog along for some incredible shopping. High Park is another favorite, really pretty, lots of scenery and off-leash areas." A perennial favorite of dog owners is Berczy Park, located in the Old Toronto district; its elegant, classical fountain is topped with a golden dog bone. The average day finds Torontonians of all stripes sitting, walking, and snapping photos next to the twenty-seven dog statues throughout the park. "The Flatiron pub is across the street," continued Ingrid. "The restaurant is underground, down a set of stairs. So the staff in the restaurant is looking outside at street level, and they have a habit of popping out dog treats as dogs wander past. All the dogs know to stop there. They walk up to the window, and poof! Out comes a treat."

The best aspect of Toronto may be that everyone seems to love dogs, even if they don't have one themselves. "I once contacted a senior home that was looking for some engaging programming," Ingrid shared. "They didn't have a ton of resources, but we thought it would be fun to do a little fashion show. So I brought Chino and whatever little bits of clothing I had, and had him become a runway model for the residents. Chino is a hundred-pound bulldog, by the way, and there he was, prancing around in these silly outfits, getting all these pets. I think it brought everybody a lot of joy."

Dining options abound in Toronto, and this includes options for diners with four-legged friends along for the meal. "The St. Lawrence Market area has always been especially dog-friendly, particularly the restaurant HotHouse," Ingrid observed. "NomNomNom café on Parliament, which recently changed its name to Playground, even had a resident dog at the café—all of their branding was based on him. And they allow you to bring your dog inside, actually. Most breweries are great with letting dogs on the patio all year round. They go out of their way to bring your dog water, or whatever else they need. Another favorite of mine is COPS donuts, and although dogs aren't allowed inside, whenever I ask for a little 'doggy bag' of donuts without frosting, they are so happy to provide it. At AAA Bar, because they don't serve food, you can take your dog inside. There are always a couple dogs in there whenever I have come by."

Many visitors use Toronto as a base to explore the smaller vacation towns of Ontario, especially in the summer months for canoeing and kayaking on glittering lakes, or wine tasting in little country villages. "Prince Edward County is a particular hotspot," Ingrid continued. "They have a lot of dog-friendly places to stay, and lots of wineries and cafés that are pet-friendly. It's about a three- or four-hour drive away and is great in the spring and summer."

Kawartha Lakes, just an hour and a half outside the city, is a favorite holiday destination for Toronto locals. The vacation town offers a plethora of resorts and hotels that are eager to welcome your dog. The Viamede Resort, built in the late 1800s and retaining much of its Victorian charm, sits on Stony Lake and welcomes pets in its vacation cottages at no extra charge. Dogs are offered treats from the front desk "cookie jar," and can enjoy a shaded, dedicated off-leash park right on the resort premises.

"However," Ingrid noted, "for visitors coming to Toronto or its surrounding vacation towns, it's a good idea to check ahead of time with your hotel about the rules for bringing your dog, even if they are pet-friendly. Sometimes the hotels are pet-friendly, but you aren't allowed to leave your dog unattended, or they'll require a crate, or extra fees. So be sure to ask your accommodations ahead of time about this. It's fairly easy to hire people to sit in the hotel with your dog while you go out, if needed."

One great reason to visit Toronto with your dog in the summer is to attend Woofstock. Held annually in late May or early June, it is North America's largest festival for dogs, attracting tens of thousands of attendees for a quirky weekend of contests, fashion shows, and agility courses and a celebration of all things canine. "I have been taking Chino since he was a puppy," Ingrid concluded. "I absolutely love it and people come from all over the world to attend. It is definitely something all pet owners should check out."

INGRID CASTRO is the proud mom of Chino and founder of Toronto Dog Moms, a community that brings together like-minded pet owners and their pups to connect and inspire each other. Toronto Dog Moms hosts dog-friendly events, sells accessories, and provides pet owners in the Toronto area with information and local news. The business also donates a portion of all sales to local rescues and humane societies, supports community GoFundMe pages, features local dog-couture vendors, and shares education on training, pet first aid, and more. You can find them on Facebook and Instagram at @TorontoDogMoms.

If You Go

▶ **Getting There:** Toronto is served by several airlines, and is the primary hub for Air Canada (888-247-2262; aircanada.com).

▶ **Best Time to Visit:** Late spring and early fall have temperate weather, but the best (and most crowded) season is probably summer, when the sidewalks come alive and patios are the most pleasant.

▶ **Accommodations:** The Hazelton Hotel (416-963-6300; thehazeltonhotel.com) and the Viamede Resort (800-461-1946; viamede.com) are bookable year-round.

▶ **Supplies:** Toronto has a number of pet stores; one favorite is Pet Mama (416-901-6262; petmama.ca).

BEND

RECOMMENDED BY **Dani Reese**

Resting against the eastern slopes of the Cascade Mountains in central Oregon, Bend boasts a dry, sunny climate where cool mountain breezes meld with the scent of high desert sage and juniper to create an intoxicating perfume. Bend's array of outdoor opportunities is second to none, ranging from golf to hiking; mountain and road biking to fly-fishing; rafting, kayaking, and stand-up paddleboarding to downhill and cross-country skiing. Many come here to vacation, and no small number end up staying. For the outdoors-oriented citizen, an argument could be made that one is *always* on vacation when living in Bend.

"Bend is a great place to visit, or live, with your dog for so many reasons," Dani Reese began. "With our high desert climate, it's frequently dry and sunny. Visit Bend, the city's travel arm, boasts of three hundred days of sunshine a year. There are so many dog-friendly trails, both on-leash and off-; many are accessible in the winter. Most of the businesses in Bend are dog-friendly, and so are the breweries and patio areas of restaurants. In the winter, you can almost always find snow in the Cascades, but to the east of town the ground is bare and dry. You can go for a ski in the morning and take a run off-leash in the afternoon."

Mount Bachelor is a major ski destination in Oregon, drawing downhillers and snowboarders from far and wide for its challenging terrain and 3,300-plus feet of vertical elevation. Dogs may not be able to slalom, but they're welcome to play, as there's a groomed play area for pooches. "You can throw a toy with your dog between runs," Dani added. (Dogs are also welcome to ride the Pine Marten chairlift in the summer with a full-body harness and can enjoy the mountain's hiking trails.) If cross-country skiing or snowshoeing is more your speed, greater Bend has a number of snow parks that welcome dogs.

One favorite is Wanoga Sno-Park, which offers some groomed trails. Edison Butte Sno-Park is also dog-friendly. The ski/snowshoe trails here double as great trail-running spots in the warmer months. If you and your pup want a nice run or bike ride in the winter, Dani recommends the Horse Butte Trail, east of town.

The summer months—at least in town and to the immediate east—might get a little too warm for some dogs to be running hard. That's when it's time to take to the river. "The Deschutes provides lots of options for getting out on the water," Dani continued. "I like to take my dog out on a stand-up paddleboard. We'll drop in the river at the main put-in right in town and head upriver to get away from the crowds." Many trails follow the Deschutes, allowing river access. If there's an angler in your group, the lower Deschutes (about an hour north of Bend) and many of region's lakes offer excellent fishing. Many guides will not mind a well-behaved dog in the boat.

Bend boasts a number of lodging options that are welcoming to dogs. One spot that affords great access to Bend's outdoor amenities while still being close to town is LOGE Bend, an outpost of LOGE Camp. "It's just west of downtown, on the Cascade Lakes highway," Dani described, "and it's very outdoor-centric. You're very close to some great biking and hiking trails, and they rent outdoors equipment for humans and dogs." LOGE offers dog beds, bowls, leashes, and harnesses from Ruffwear (which is based in Bend) to make your pup's stay comfortable. Two- and four-legged parties will enjoy a leisurely drive on the Cascade Lakes Scenic Byway, which passes twelve lakes as it winds past various Cascades peaks and highlights a host of geological wonders. Many trails adjoin the highway, and the lakes beckon swimmers, canoers, and paddleboarders alike. Some of the lakes (including Elk Lake and Lava Lake) feature old-time resorts offering respite from the road in the form of an ice cream cone or a rowboat rental.

Like Portland to the west, Bend is a beer lover's nirvana, with one brewery for every 4,500 residents. Most are very dog-friendly. Bend Brewing Company, right in the center of town above the Mirror Pond section of the Deschutes River, has a large fenced-in area for dogs to ramble in while you enjoy a libation. Crux Fermentation Project, near the Old Mill neighborhood, has a large lawn, food carts, live music, inspiring Cascades views, and some of Oregon's most inventive beers.

Often in this life, the stars may not align to provide the existence we hope for. But sometimes, if we persevere, things do come together . . . as they did for Dani. "I first applied for a job with Ruffwear in 2012, but nothing came of it. I tried again in 2018, and

OPPOSITE:
The Cascade
Lakes Scenic
Byway near
Bend provides
access to many
mountain lakes.

DESTINATION

33

found a fit. I'll never forget meeting up with some fellow Ruffwear employees with my dog at two thirty in the morning for a trail run to the top of South Sister, an incredible snowcapped volcano just west of town. To see the sunrise from the mountain and then run back to town to make it to the office by eight thirty for a company meeting with my fellow employees and my dog—this was the life I'd always wanted to live."

DANI REESE is the community manager at Ruffwear, an outdoor performance dog gear company based in Bend, Oregon. She grew up competing in running and eventually earned a scholarship to Appalachian State University in Boone, North Carolina, where her love for the outdoors and the mountains grew. After competing in Division I athletics for four years, she moved across the country to Portland, Oregon, and has called the Pacific Northwest home for the past ten years (excluding a short stint managing a hostel in Slovakia, complete with a hostel dog). These days you can find her trail running, backpacking, and skiing with her pine cone–obsessed dog, Vilas, who accompanies her to work every day.

If You Go

DESTINATION

33

▶ **Getting There:** Visitors to Bend can fly into nearby Redmond Municipal Airport, which is served by several carriers, including Alaska Airlines (800-252-7522; alaskaair.com). Portland International Airport (3.5 hours from Bend by car) is served by most major carriers.

▶ **Best Time to Visit:** Bend is a true four-season resort, though it's probably busiest in the summer months. You can generally rely on a good deal of sunshine whenever you visit.

▶ **Accommodations:** There are almost fifty hotel properties in Bend that welcome pets; Visit Bend (877.245.8484; visitbend.com) provides a current list. LOGE Bend (541-306-3111; logecamps.com) is well situated for outdoor activities.

▶ **Supplies:** Bend has a number of stores serving your dog's needs, including Bendy Dog (661-305-2466; bendydog.com) and Mud Bay (541-306-2660; mudbay.com).

PORTLAND

RECOMMENDED BY **Lanette Fidrych**

Portland rests at the confluence of the Columbia and Willamette Rivers, at the northern end of Oregon's Willamette Valley. For many years, Portland lived in the shadow of its flashier neighbors, San Francisco and Seattle, quietly walking its own walk. But in the past few decades, the city's proximity to the dramatic Oregon coast and the recreational opportunities of the Cascade Mountains and Columbia River Gorge, its thriving foodie culture, and its progressive aura have thrust it into the limelight. Given its abundance of green space, its accessibility to the countryside, and a dog-positive attitude that welcomes dogs in many retail stores (and just about every restaurant with an outdoor area), most canines would agree that Portland is a great place to live . . . or visit.

Lanette Fidrych's experience in launching her business, Cycle Dog, captures the gestalt of Portland's puppy scene. "Before Cycle Dog, I was working at Nike [in nearby Beaverton]," she began. "I would bike to work and, inevitably, would get flat tires. I started saving the punctured tubes, thinking I could make something out of them. I had two labs at the time, so I began building dog leashes. The first few exploded. But over time, I figured out a way to make a pretty good product, and I gave them away to friends. Some said, 'These are great, you should make a business out of this.' I didn't know anything about starting a business. But I made a bunch of leashes and attended some farmers' markets around town. The leashes sold out quickly. Pet stores around town started calling, hoping to carry the product. So suddenly, I was in business."

One of Portland's greatest assets for dogs (and dog walkers) is Forest Park. The park abuts the city's northwest quadrant and stretches seven miles above the Willamette River, boasting more than eighty miles of soft-surface trails, fire lanes, and forest roads. At over five thousand acres, it is considered the largest urban forest in the United States. "I can

walk out the door of my house and be in the park in a few minutes," Lanette continued. "Sometimes people ask me how I can live in a city with four dogs. Having Forest Park so nearby makes it possible. On weekdays, Wildwood Trail is our first choice. It's not congested, there are many entry points, and it goes on forever. On weekends or busier times, I like the Holman Lane trail, also in Forest Park. It's a nice wide trail and it's a little more off the beaten path." Portland offers dogs more than 150 other parks, many with off-leash or fenced-in play areas.

Portland is one of America's craft-brewing hotspots, with roughly seventy breweries/ brewpubs within the city limits. That, and the region's occasionally dreary weather, has created a thriving pub culture. Dogs are welcome at many. "For lots of Portland dog owners, if you get a new puppy, the first thing you do is take it to your local pub to show it off!" Lanette enthused. "A few favorites include Breakside Brewery, Gigantic, StormBreaker, and Great Notion. Lucky Labrador, one of Portland's older brewpubs, has held Dogtoberfest each September since 1995, with live music, a special brew, and a dog wash to raise funds for a local emergency animal hospital, DoveLewis. To date, more than eight thousand dogs have been washed, raising more than $130,000."

Lanette described how an ideal Portland dog day might evolve: "I'd start with a walk down to Dragonfly Coffee House. You can get coffee to go, or sit with your pooch at an outside table. Then we might hit the Wildwood Trail for a little nature. Lunch would be at Breakside Brewery's Northwest Portland location. They have a big outside patio, excellent beer, and are great about having dogs around. After lunch, we might take a stroll to Washington Park and Portland's famous rose garden—there's a large dog-friendly area. Alternatively, we could do some window shopping on Northwest Twenty-Third; a majority of the businesses allow dogs inside and supply treats. We might finish the day at the Cycle Dog Tavern. It's completely dog-friendly; there are human beverages, from kombucha to beer, and indoor and outdoor dog parks."

Portland has built a reputation as a city that's friendly to dogs. As Lanette has learned, it's also a close community of friendly dog owners. "There was a brewpub in northwest Portland named Old Lompoc [now closed] that we used to visit often," she recalled. "We'd often see a woman there who would foster dogs in need of adoption. I took a liking to one dog that she was fostering, and week after week I'd see it there. I couldn't figure out why this dog wasn't getting adopted, as he was adorable. One visit, she mentioned that she was going to have to go out of town for a while, and was going to have to bring the dog back

OPPOSITE:
Portlanders
(and their dogs)
never let a little
misty weather
interrupt with
walks through
Forest Park.

DESTINATION

34

155

to the shelter. I adopted that dog from the brewery patio, and he was with us for six or seven years.

"At one point, we had four dogs. One was an older Lab that was unable to get around very well. When we'd go out for walks, we'd bring along a little wagon, the kind you might use in your yard. She'd be able to walk with the other dogs a few blocks; when she got tired, we'd put her in the wagon. So we'd be walking along with three dogs on a leash and one in the wagon, and no one thought it at all odd. People we passed would smile, seeing how happy she was to be out and about. We'd often roll her down to the Dragonfly and get her a peanut butter cookie. The baristas working there used to say that having my Lab roll up in her wagon was something they'd wait for all morning, the best part of their day."

LANETTE FIDRYCH is the founder and CEO of Cycle Dog (cycledog.com) in Portland, Oregon, a company she launched after a successful career at Nike. Cycle Dog started with collars made of recycled inner tubes, and has expanded to include a host of other products. Adjacent to its showroom, Cycle Dog operates a dog-friendly tavern and indoor/ outdoor dog parks. A dog, beer, and biking enthusiast, Lanette resides in Portland with her dogs, Maggie, Hannah, and Mr. Sneaky.

DESTINATION
34

If You Go

► **Getting There:** Portland International Airport is served by most major carriers.
► **Best Time to Visit:** You'll find the most reliable weather from June through mid-October, though temperatures are clement throughout the year. Dogtoberfest is generally held in mid-September.
► **Accommodations:** Travel Portland (800-962-3700; travelportland.com) lists a number of hotels that welcome dogs. These include McMenamins Kennedy School Hotel (503-249-3983; mcmenamins.com/kennedy-school), a former elementary school that's been transformed into a pub/restaurant/hotel.
► **Supplies:** Portland is awash in stores purveying dog supplies. A few include Mud Bay (mudbay.com) and Green Dog Pet Supply (503-528-1800; greendogpetsupply.com).

PHILADELPHIA

RECOMMENDED BY **Curtis Kelley**

Philadelphia is celebrated for its Revolutionary history, annual Mummers Parade, and inventing one of America's most beloved sandwiches. The City of Brotherly Love, however, is equally friendly to is canine citizens.

"Dog culture in Philly is strong," Curtis Kelley observed. "There are a lot of people who are really, really dedicated to their dogs. People hike with their dogs, take their dogs to happy hour. They get dogs with the intention of folding them into their lives, not to leave at home."

Philadelphia's park system is a great boon for dog owners. In many metropolises, going for a hike with your dog means driving *out* of the city. This is not the case in Philadelphia, where in-city parks resemble forests and span miles. "There are three major spots for hiking," continued Curtis, "The first and the biggest is Wissahickon Valley Park. There are hundreds of miles of trails inside of it; it's hard to believe you're in a city. Then there's Fairmount Park, which weaves through a long stretch of the city. There are some areas with tea and meditation houses, and historic buildings you bump into on the way. The last of the 'big ones' is Roosevelt Park, which is just a gorgeous, open, grassy loop—three to four miles total if you do the whole thing."

Generally speaking, dogs should be on-leash while out and about. Where leashes aren't required, the expectation is that your dog is under voice control. "It's a common scenario you'll run into. My wife and I were walking with Vista, our doberman, one day, and we saw someone approach with a dog off-leash. What happens then is people generally ask if you're okay with that, and if you say you're not (we said no, because Vista is not great in that situation), they are courteous and put their dog on-leash. It didn't always used to be that way, and it's not that way in every city. But it's really wonderful that this conscientiousness is becoming a normal part of our dog culture."

If your pup tires of walking the city's lush parks, consider a carriage ride. A handful of charming horse-drawn buggies often wait for customers at Independence Mall. Nicknamed "America's Most Historic Square," this is the home of the Liberty Bell and Independence Hall, where the Declaration of Independence was drafted and signed. Stroll the park's manicured grounds with your pup and then hop into a buggy for a ride to dinner (while many buggy drivers are used to having a canine aboard, be sure to ask first before hopping in).

"After a walk, my wife and I would often visit Goose Island Brewhouse [now closed] with some other friends who have dogs," reflected Curtis. "It was attached to a comedy club, and they had a fully enclosed yard, with lots of firepits. It was the kind of place where dogs could run around, stretch their legs a little, while you sat and had a beer and chitchatted with friends. On one visit, we met up for a training session, and it was just pouring rain, total downpour. We were easily the only people there in the back. The staff thought we were silly for sitting outside. But they brought out space heaters, and were really kind about making us comfortable. Vista and Fennel were under a year old at that time, and they couldn't really focus on anything because of the rain, so we figured training was a bust and let them off-leash. They were darting and diving under the tables like it was an obstacle course. Then they came up and shook off the mud onto our table *just* as the staff brought out our food. We were mortified. But the staff just thought it was hilarious; they brought us some fresh burgers. I was really impressed by their kindness."

Other local dog-friendly favorites include Wissahickon Brewing Company, with its spacious outdoor patio, and the aptly named White Dog Cafe, which serves upscale American cuisine to humans and ensures each canine visitor has their own water bowl. Rouge, the first restaurant in Philly to offer sidewalk seating so that guests might better enjoy the view of Rittenhouse Square, offers complimentary treats to visiting pups. A recent favorite can be found at Craft Hall, where the combined restaurant and dog park known as Unleashed: Bark & Beer allows dogs to roam free on the enclosed two-thousand-square-foot puppy porch. Dogs can order their heart's desire from a menu of treats, while their owners sip a craft cocktail or beer.

Philadelphia is a foodie city, so a touch of caution should be exercised when walking the streets with your dog. "I don't know if this is true for other cities, but chicken bones seem to rain from the sky here," Curtis warned. "Be sure to check the ground wherever you walk. In Philly, there's a spot on every corner that does wings, and the bones don't always make it into the trash can."

OPPOSITE: Wissahickon Valley Park is a popular arboreal escape in the City of Brotherly Love, offering hundreds of miles of trails.

DESTINATION 35

When it's time to rest, visitors shouldn't have trouble finding a pet-friendly hotel. Some notables include the Kimpton Hotel Palomar, who employ their very own "Director of Pet Relations," a dachshund named Vienna. Aloft Philadelphia Downtown's "Arf Package," is complimentary for every canine guest, and includes bedding, food, water bowls, and treats. There are also grassy spots on-site where your pooch can do their business.

"Culturally, Philly is a very active dog owner city," Curtis concluded. "There is a lot to do here with you and your dog."

CURTIS KELLEY, CPDT-KA, is the owner of Pet Parent Allies. He offers private training sessions and companion selection consults in Philadelphia, Pennsylvania. He works with reactivity, aggression, and obedience and offers unique solutions for urban dog owners. Curtis also sits on the board of directors for the Association of Professional Dog Trainers (APDT), where he is working to bring more diversity into the dog training field. When he's not training, Curtis enjoys gardening, reading, and hiking with his wife, Karen, and their doberman, Vista. You can learn more at petparentallies.com; find him on Instagram at @petparenteducation_CPDTKA and on Facebook at facebook.com/petparentalliesphilly.

If You Go

▶ **Getting There:** Philadelphia International Airport is the hub of American Airlines (800-433-7300; aa.com).

▶ **Best Time to Visit:** Summer is popular, but the heat can be sweltering. March to May sees the parks in bloom and more moderate temperatures.

▶ **Accommodations:** The Kimpton Hotel Palomar Philadelphia (215-563-5006; hotel palomar-philadelphia.com) and Aloft Philadelphia Downtown (215-607-2020; marriott .com) can be booked year-round; be sure to mention your dog at booking. The city's official tourism website, Visit Philadelphia (visitphilly.com), has lists of reliable hotels.

▶ **Supplies:** Monster Pets (215-336-9000; monsterpetsonline.com) is a South Philly favorite, selling toys, gear, and treats and offering large self-service grooming tubs with pressure-controlled hoses.

ALJEZUR

RECOMMENDED BY **Alyson Sheldrake**

"The western part of the Algarve hasn't been affected by tourism as much as other places in the region," Alyson Sheldrake began. "The first time we came here, we rented a small fisherman's cottage in Ferragudo. As we entered the village, we turned the corner, and bam— there was the harbor, whitewashed houses, a little church, a sparkling blue river leading to the ocean, and traditional painted boats clanking in the breeze. This part of Portugal is so wonderful. It's the way of life, the people, the food that make it so special. We quickly bought a house in Ferragudo and moved here to live in 2011. That gave me the chance to do something I always wanted to do as an adult, which was to have a rescue dog."

The Iberian attitude toward dogs is mixed. In cities, dogs are often pampered. In the country, they are more appreciated for their labor value. "There are a lot of strays and abandoned dogs in Spain and Portugal. Farm dogs are often tied up outside to stand guard for the sheep and chickens," Alyson said. "They sometimes are seen as no more important than a chicken." However, there are also many rescue groups and charity organizations that provide for street dogs and help place them in new homes. "We had a friend, Ginie, who worked for a local charity, and she saw a dog on the side of the road in just a pitiful state— ticks, fleas, underweight, everything," Alyson described. "She stopped initially to give her some food and water. But when she opened her car door, the stray just jumped in. Ginie posted a photo of her online and the moment I saw her, and I knew right then, that was my girl. Dave named her Kat and we fell in love with her the day we met her.

"We moved to live in Aljezur on the west coast four years ago. On our morning walks beside the river, Kat is rarely on a lead. I always have one, but she never needs one," Alyson explained. "And where we live is such an open rural area. Aljezur is a very small and friendly community. Of the thirty houses in our little hamlet, about fifteen families have dogs, and most of them are the family pet. Which is not what you see everywhere in Portugal."

The Aljezur area is rich with history. A tenth-century Moorish castle sits high on a hill overlooking the town, built upon an Iron Age castrum and a Roman watchtower. The Alfambres and Cercal Rivers, once vast trade channels, join at Aljezur and travel west to meet the Atlantic Ocean at Praia da Amoreira. "Every morning, Kat and I walk down to the river together," Alyson continued. "There's nobody else around. All you hear is the birds singing in the trees and the poplar trees rustling. Often you can see otters, pond turtles, and white storks. There's a little café about halfway round the walk, and the owner has the local geese so tame, he just whistles and they come waddling up from the riverbank and eat out of his hand."

One side of the river is industrial farmland, but on the other side, most of the families tend their own vegetable plots. "Our neighbors often knock on our door, gifting us their fresh fruit and vegetables," Alyson said. "Everyone helps each other. One neighbor has a mule and an old-fashioned plow, and the mule tills the soil in the fields. One of my neighbors cooks her rabbit stew in the same cauldron that her great-grandmother used. She lights an open fire and hangs it on a hook. The cauldron is probably one hundred twenty years old."

No trip to the Algarve would be complete without a visit to the area's famous coastline. "It will always be clearly signed if your dog isn't allowed on a beach, and in the summertime, these signs will be displayed on the main beaches," Alyson advised. "But you really wouldn't want to take them on the sand in the summer, anyway—it gets too hot. As the weather cools, the beach empties, the lifeguard stations are dismantled, and you can walk your dog on the beach again."

In the Algarve, there are so many off-the-beaten-path areas that it isn't hard to find a welcoming place for you and your pup. Consider a visit to Praia Grande beach at Ferragudo, especially at low tide, when you can stroll through open coves, watch flocks of seagulls take flight, and meander to the Farol do Molhe lighthouse and back. "There are several beaches within five minutes of Aljezur, but Kat's favorite is Monte Clérigo," Alyson continued. "The minute we open the car door, she's gone, straight down to the sand, pure joy on her face. There are lots of rock pools to explore, and there's a lovely little café there, where you can sit out and watch the beach. The staff always come out and bring her a treat. They call her 'little sheep' or 'little monkey' in Portuguese. Everybody knows her."

One note: If you come in spring, be aware of ticks (which can be avoided with a standard-issue tick collar) and pine processionary caterpillars, (which can prove to be very dangerous for the unwitting canine—and human!)

"Around Aljezur, you can pretty much go anywhere with your dog," Alyson concluded. "The Portuguese are very friendly; we have several restaurants that welcome Kat inside. But of course, it hardly matters out here, because you usually want to eat outside and enjoy the incredible weather. If you've got a dog, it's just a great place to travel or live."

ALYSON SHELDRAKE is an author, an artist, and the proud mom of Kat the Dog. Her art style emphasizes new wave landscapes, seascapes, and pet portraits. She is the author of the Algarve Dream series and the author/curator of the Travel Stories series. Her latest book, *Kat the Dog: The Remarkable Tale of a Rescued Spanish Water Dog*, was released in May 2022. Alyson has an honors degree in sport, and spent thirteen years working as a police officer before leaving the force to rapidly work her way up the ranks of the education advisory service to become a director of education. Together with her husband, Dave, a professional photographer, she left the dreary, gray British weather in 2011 and set up her art studio in the beautiful, sunny Algarve in Portugal.

If You Go

▶ **Getting There:** The airport nearest to Aljezur is Faro, the gateway airport for the Algarve, which is served by RyanAir (ryanair.com) and TAP (800-221-7370; flytap.com).

▶ **Best Time to Visit:** September and October offer quieter beaches and balmy evenings, as well as less-crowded beaches. Consider avoiding March and April, the height of tick and caterpillar season.

▶ **Accommodations:** There are a handful of dog-friendly hotels in Aljezur and the surrounding beaches. The Algarve tourism board lists accommodations at visitalgarve.pt/en. Or check out nearby Aldeia da Pedralva (+351 282 639 342; aldeiadapedralva.com/en), a wonderful eco-village where you can stay in a renovated traditional Portuguese house.

▶ **Supplies:** In town, Fertizur (+351 282 995 460; fertizur.pt) is a hardware and farm store that also carries a large variety of pet foods and gear.

LISBON

RECOMMENDED BY **Luís de Andrade Peixoto**

Luís de Andrade Peixoto became a dog owner at a time when Portugal's attitudes about dogs were evolving in a positive direction. "People have grown more sensitive about how they treat dogs and pets," he said. "New generations of Portuguese are much more aware of animals, that our pets are beings. Circuses no longer are permitted to have animals as part of the show, and the existence of zoos is being called into question. There's even talk of stopping bullfighting, which is a huge tradition here.

"We see the change in how the society treats street dogs. They used to have a bad association," Luís continued. "But in the last ten or fifteen years, the government is picking them up, and encouraging adoption. There are many initiatives—both private and from city councils—to sponsor shelters. There are even ad campaigns urging people to adopt dogs instead of buying them. As awareness of pets increases, there's been a movement to create more pet-friendly spaces—both among businesses and public spaces. Not so long ago, you couldn't bring a dog to the beach; now there are more and more beaches where you can bring animals. We adopted Lucky, our sweet podengo—a popular and long-established breed on the Iberian Peninsula—in 2018. Our timing was good."

If you ever peruse travel magazines, you've likely come upon glowing reviews of Lisbon, Portugal's capital city, resting on the north banks of the river Tagus. Lisbon gracefully blends a rich history and centuries-old traditions with a thriving cultural and gastronomic scene (it's not just *bacalhau* anymore, though variations of salted cod are not difficult to find). And it doesn't hurt that Lisbon boasts a mild climate with nearly three hundred days of sunshine a year, and beautiful beaches within a short drive or train ride from downtown. Lisbon, and Portugal in general, has largely overcome the

DESTINATION

37

economic hardships of the 2000s and 2010s, and are attracting émigrés from the rest of Europe and beyond.

"It seems that everyone has discovered Portugal," Luís said. "*Condé Nast Traveler* has named it one of the top five or ten destinations. Lisbon has done a wonderful job balancing the traditional with the dynamics of museums and upscale restaurants—it's very cosmopolitan. Many people are moving from America, China, Paris—and the art scene, which is exploding, reflects this. I think that the international presence in Lisbon has impacted the dynamics of how we interact with our dogs. At one time, it was common for people who owned dogs to walk them in the morning before work and then in the evening before going to bed. Now it's completely impossible to think about our pets that way. My partner and I are both freelancers, and work from home. I'd say we're able to walk Lucky three hours a day—in the morning, after lunch, and after dinner. You can bring dogs to the office, to meetings, even to many art galleries. If you're invited out, your pet is invited, too. Lucky is with us all the time."

Any discussion of Lisbon will soon turn to its food and wine offerings. "We have a huge and complex gastronomic tradition, with many differences from north to south," Luís observed. "Of course, given our huge coastline, we have very fresh shellfish and fish. Cod is the favorite ingredient from the sea, but octopus and sardines are also quite popular." Hams, sausages, and other pork products are also mainstays. A few of Luís's favorite dishes include *arroz de marisco* (a seafood and rice dish, often featuring shellfish); *frango assado* (grilled chicken, usually served with french fries and rice); *sardinhas assadas* (grilled sardines); *bacalhau à brás* (which combines salt cod, potatoes and eggs); and *cozido à portuguesa* (a stew of slow-cooked meats, sausages, and vegetables).

The wines of Portugal are also garnering great attention—and we're not talking just about port (a fortified sweet red wine). "A huge percentage of our wines are now being exported, maybe eighty to eighty-five percent of production," Luís explained. "Our wines are winning awards, but I think it's really because of the wave of tourism we've seen. People are enjoying our wines when they visit and seeking them out when they return home. In the north, vintners are making some great rosés and fine sparkling wines, too."

Lisbon's dynamic gastro scene can increasingly be enjoyed with your dog by your side. "From posh to more modest restaurants, there are more and more spaces where you can bring your dog," Luís added. A few of his picks for dog-friendly eateries include

DESTINATION

37

Tamariz (in Estoril); Borda d'Água (in Costa da Caparica); and Manifest and Kaffeehaus, both in Lisbon proper.

As mentioned earlier, Lisbon's proximity to the Atlantic and its fine beaches is a definite perk, and more and more beaches are carving out space for canine visitors. "The beaches are one reason people go crazy for Lisbon," Luís said. "Some are only twenty-five minutes by train from downtown; others, just a bit further, though you'll need to drive. They are close enough you can go to the beach in the morning and easily make it home in time to attend a work meeting in the afternoon. Lucky gets very relaxed at the beach. He doesn't like going into the water, but will make a hole in the sand and sleep for hours with just his nose sticking up, smelling the breeze." A few dog-friendly beaches Luís recommends include Praia Irmão and Praia da Bela Vista at Costa da Caparica, south of where the Tagus joins the Atlantic; and Praia do Tamariz at Estoril, just north of the estuary.

Dogs and high fashion don't generally reside in intersecting circles. But in Lisbon, Luís has found a tolerance for canines in unexpected places. "Not long after we got Lucky, there was a store opening for a fashion designer we knew," he recalled. "We hadn't taken Lucky out for many social events, but we decided to go. It was a very posh store with all the big fashion brands—Chanel, Gucci, et cetera. Traditionally, it was a space that you wouldn't take a dog to. But everyone was crazy about Lucky. Since then, we've taken her to art gallery openings, fashion stores, and art fairs. After attending such events, Lucky has had his photo in fashion and art magazines."

LUÍS DE ANDRADE PEIXOTO is founder of the brand Moove Up—Worldwide Strategy, a communication and consultancy firm that manages a complex range of projects for clients, brands, and institutions from Portugal, Spain, the UK, France, Sweden, Italy, Brazil, Angola, and Japan. Passionate about arts and history, he has a master's degree in museum studies and is involved in many cultural and art projects. Currently, one of his main projects is JustLX—Lisboa Contemporary Art Fair, which is focused on emerging artists and new art dynamics in Lisbon and Madrid.

If You Go

▶ **Getting There:** Many carriers serve Lisbon from the United States, including TAP (800-221-7370; flytap.com).

▶ **Best Time to Visit:** Lisbon has a generally mild climate year-round. Beachgoers will appreciate summer and early fall; visitors seeking cooler temperatures will enjoy springtime.

▶ **Accommodations:** You'll find a complete list of dog-friendly hotels at bringfido.com.

▶ **Supplies:** There are a number of shops for your dog in Lisbon, including Pets Closet (+351 935 108 530; petscloset.pt) and Perfect Pet (+351 21 394 0605; www.perfectpet.pt).

DESTINATION

37

MONTREAL

RECOMMENDED BY **Mai Tran**

Canada's City of Saints is best known for its internationally acclaimed festivals, vibrant art networks, and multicultural food scene (but don't forget to grab a box of traditional poutine before you leave town). "The dog culture has been developing more and more with each passing year," Mai Tran observed. "Montreal downtown is the most dog-friendly area. It has the best pet boutiques, best restaurants, and is where most of the dogs are hanging out. And outside of the city, the nature is incredible, especially in the summer."

Montreal is a highly walkable city, especially downtown, where many residents forgo owning a car. With this high walkability comes a natural dog-friendliness, including an abundance of parks and shop owners happy to welcome a well-behaved pup inside. "We really like walking around Old Port of Montreal, and Saint-Laurent Boulevard, but especially rue Sainte-Catherine," reflected Mai. "The street runs through downtown, and there are loads of little shops and boutiques, and almost all are dog-friendly." While strolling the famous main street of Montreal's downtown, consider visiting the grounds of the Notre-Dame Basilica, built in the 1800s to hold up to ten thousand of Canada's French Catholic immigrants and considered a masterpiece of neo-Gothic architecture. Visit inside for an even more impressive light show (although Fido will have to wait outside with a friend). "The restaurants in the downtown area are very dog-friendly, for the most part," continued Mai. "A good rule of thumb is that just about any place with a patio will be happy to have you and your dog. I'm a big brunch person, and we particularly like Ruby's Café. It's part of Doggieville Mtl, which is a doggy day care and grooming salon. The café is wonderful, and it's a place where you really feel particularly welcome."

Cross the Samuel De Champlain Bridge to depart downtown and experience the Quartier DIX30 mall, with its bevvy of spas, boutiques, art installations, and rooftop

*OPPOSITE:
Fairy-tale
lavender fields
just outside
Montreal make
for a wonderful
day trip for dogs
and humans
alike.*

DESTINATION

38

patios. "That's probably the most dog-friendly neighborhood in the whole city," continued Mai. "There's water bowls everywhere and complimentary waste bags. It's one of those neighborhoods where everywhere you look, everyone has a dog."

Montreal is considered one of the most world's livable cities, thanks in part to its abundant green spaces and public gardens. Depending on the season, you can hike, snowshoe, canoe, and even toboggan all within the official city boundary. The most famous of the in-city parks is Mont Royal. Sometimes simply referred to as "the mountain," the landscape was designed by Frederick Law Olmsted (who designed New York's Central Park, among other projects). Mont Royal features nearly five hundred acres of green grass, native flora and fauna, boat rides on Beaver Lake, and plays host to Montreal's massive weekly Sunday gathering of drummers, dancers, and vendors called Les Tam-tams. "It's an incredible space that rises up on the northern part of the island," Mai said. "And even better, it's an off-leash park. It's very popular with dogs, especially in the summertime. Our favorite place is Summit Woods, on the tail end of the park. It's very green, like a proper forest. It's hard to remember you're in the middle of a city."

Summer may be the most glorious time to visit Montreal, as that's when the city hosts most of its internationally renowned festivals. If your furry friend enjoys music, the Montreal International Jazz Festival cannot be beat. The event, which typically takes place the first week of July, transforms the Quartier des Spectacles into the world's biggest jazz club, with more than five hundred shows, many of which are outdoors. If comedy is more to your taste, consider visiting during the comedy festival Juste Pour Rire ("Just for Laughs"), which is held near the end of May and is one of the largest comedy festivals in the world. "Both of those festivals are very dog-friendly and a lot of the content is outdoors," noted Mai.

Many visitors will want to explore Quebec's countryside, and many destinations are just a short drive from downtown. "For hiking, we really love Diable Vert, a spectacularly beautiful forest area," described Mai. "I'm not an advanced hiker, and neither is Herky [her Cavalier King Charles spaniel], but it's a perfect, accessible space with leisurely, well-marked trails. And it's only thirty-five to forty minutes southwest of the city." In the fall, head west out of Montreal to visit the Centre d'Interpretation de la Courge pumpkin patch, and enjoying roaming the vines with Fido in search of the perfect jack-o'-lantern. Or head east and visit the Petit et Fils cider house and apple orchard, which has fifty thousand trees and welcomes dogs for a pleasant afternoon of apple picking and wandering the orchard's acres of fragrant fruiting trees.

"A favorite place of ours on the North Shore, just outside of the city is La Maison Lavande," Mai shared. "It's spectacular during the summer when it's nice and hot. They have shaded areas, music, refreshments. You can arrive with your dog, take a walk, have a picnic, all amongst the lavender fields. It's such a relaxing atmosphere, very calming, and all the breezy lavender everywhere. A lot of people dream of going to Provence, and don't get me wrong, the lavender fields there are amazing. But you can experience that kind of splendor in Quebec.

"Montreal is a lovely city to visit with your dog," Mai concluded. "It's a hidden gem in the dog world, and there's so much you can explore together."

MAI TRAN is a lawyer, dog mom to Cavalier King Charles spaniels Herky and Milton, and CEO of Cavology, which designs haute couture dog leashes, harnesses, apparel, and more. When she's not posting training tips and designer tricks on @herkythecavalier's social channels, she's always thinking of new dog accessory designs and how to improve existing ones. Her family splits their time between Montreal and Los Angeles, and as CEO of Cavology, Mai ensures a portion of all sales go to local dog shelters and dog-centered charities. Her end goal is to one day be able to open her own dog shelter and offer dogs a second chance at a beautiful life.

If You Go

▶ **Getting There:** Montréal–Trudeau International Airport is served by many international carriers and is the hub of Air Canada (888-247-2262; aircanada.com).

▶ **Best Time to Visit:** Montreal has wonderful winter sports, but most restaurants welcome dogs on the patio only. Summer and fall are more ideal for hiking and exploring the lavender fields and orchards around Montreal.

▶ **Accommodations:** Tourism Montréal lists reliable accommodations at mtl.org.

▶ **Supplies:** Montreal has a large number of pet stores. A favorite for luxury goods and holistic foods is Boutique Pawse Inc. (514-800-9172; boutique.paws.ca).

SASKATOON

RECOMMENDED BY **Ashlyn George**

"I was always bringing animals home with me growing up," Ashlyn George began. "One time I saved a coyote pup; another time I brought home a stray cat. We didn't always get to keep them, of course. But when I met Alpine, our rescue, I fell in love immediately. She is my favorite travel companion."

Known as the "Paris of the Prairies," Saskatoon is crisscrossed by the vast South Saskatchewan River and is surrounded by acres of golden wheat fields. Like any proper northern city, it is chock-full of snow sports options, but Saskatchewan also enjoys more days of sunlight per year than any other Canadian province, making it a wonderful destination for hiking, festivals, boating, and other summer activities. The Bridge City has been steadily growing over the decades and is now a veritable cultural hub. "It is so much fun to see Saskatoon from a different perspective with a dog," continued Ashlyn. "I'm a very active person, but Alpine is an added reason to motivate me to get out and get moving."

Saskatoon has an impressive number of dog parks, from small and fenced to broad and unbounded. "One favorite of ours is the Sutherland Beach off-leash dog park, just north of the center of the city and next to the river," Ashlyn said. "It's a big open area with bikers, runners, walkers, and of course lots of dogs. There are stands of trees to explore in and really cool paths you can take, some leading right down to the river, to beautiful sandy beaches. Dogs can play there openly. It's a dream of a place, and hard to remember you're in the middle of a city."

The river is a central feature of Saskatoon, and dogs that love the water will find themselves happily at home. "Just south of the city there are several canoe launches," continued Ashlyn. "There are beaches all along the river's edge. You never have to travel far. I took Alpine to a nearby beach one afternoon. She's not really a swimmer. She'll go into

OPPOSITE:
Two traveling
companions
reflect on the
day's adventures
at the edge of
Waterhen River
in Meadow Lake
Provincial Park.

DESTINATION

39

the water to fetch a stick, but her feet won't leave the sandy bottom. It was important she knew how to swim, so we went out to Poplar Bluffs. It's a canoe launch area with a big expanse of beach. I literally picked her up in my arms and carried her into a deeper part of the water. And lo and behold, with our support, she swam. I suppose you could say it's a good place to give swim lessons, too."

If you and your dog prefer to stick to solid ground, Saskatoon can be a jumping-off point to an incredible array of trails. From numerous trailheads downtown, you can hop on a section of the sixty-five-mile Meewasin Trail, which runs along the river and is part of the Great Trail. And of course, outside Saskatoon, the national parks of the Saskatchewan backcountry await. "Hiking and camping with a dog can be an incredibly rewarding experience," reflected Ashlyn. "A few years ago, I took Alpine on a road trip to Grasslands National Park. It was April, and relatively quiet. I planned to do a hike called the Valley of 1000 Devils. It's similar topography to the Badlands in South Dakota. You can be hiking and come across dinosaur bones. But there's also not a lot of windbreaks. We set up our camp, I get into my tent and sleeping bag, and we cuddled up together. Then this insane wind whips up. It starts pushing the tent into me as I'm lying down. I'm out of cell service and I'm the only one out here. I realize I have to take my tent down before it breaks. I start emergency-stuffing everything into my backpack, trying to get my tent down so it doesn't become a parachute and blow me away with it. Coyotes were howling. It was so dark. I couldn't see anything beyond the three-foot light of my headlamp. But Alpine was there with me. She was patient, she knew something was wrong, and she stayed cool. I felt so much safer having her there as a companion. I was able to move our camp, and she came back into the tent and we snuggled together and made it through the night."

While Saskatoon is a great base camp for exploring the incredible wilderness of central Canada, the downtown area is also extremely welcoming to visiting canines. "One weekend my mom came to visit and we had a dog-friendly mother-daughter vacation. We stayed at the Alt Hotel on the fifteenth floor. It has amazing views of downtown and the river flowing through the city. They literally give you a pillow for your dog to sleep on. We visited flower shops, antiques stores, and boutiques. I discovered I could take Alpine everywhere. The exception is going inside restaurants, but in the summer, everywhere has a patio—and if there's a patio, generally your dog is welcome.

"Sometimes people call Saskatchewan 'the gap' and talk about it like there's nothing here to see," Ashlyn concluded. "But I have traveled extensively. I wanted to hit all seven continents before I turned thirty, and I did. And I love my backyard most of all. There is so much space and natural beauty. I feel so lucky, especially since I can include Alpine in almost every activity in the city. The companionship I get from her is real. So it's such a good feeling when this animal that depends on you can come with you, have a great time, and you both can have the richest experience possible."

ASHLYN GEORGE, BA, BEd, is an award-winning travel writer, photographer, and content creator behind the Lost Girl's Guide to Finding the World. She is the go-to travel expert in Saskatchewan but is no stranger to trips abroad. A passionate storyteller, she's traveled solo through more than sixty countries on all seven continents in pursuit of adventure, learning, and discovery. Find her at thelostgirlsguide.com and on Instagram at @thelostgirlsguide.

If You Go

▶ **Getting There:** Saskatoon International Airport (known as Skyxe) is served by the Canadian airlines WestJet (888-937-8538; westjet.com), Air Canada (888-247-2262; air canada.com), and Flair Airlines (833-711-2333; flyflair.com).

▶ **Best Time to Visit:** For long, sunny days, June to August is the best time to visit. December to February is the best time of year for winter sports.

▶ **Accommodations:** The Alt Hotel Saskatoon takes year-round reservations (639-398-0250; germainhotels.com/en/alt-hotel) and Tourism Saskatoon lists a variety of dog-friendly accommodations at tourismsaskatoon.com.

▶ **Supplies:** Saskatoon has numerous pet stores, but a local favorite is Critters Pet Health Store (306-665-5600; critterspet.com), which has a few locations around the city.

EDINBURGH

RECOMMENDED BY **Gareth Davies**

"Edinburgh has the highest percentage of green space of any city in the UK," Gareth Davies observed. "Almost half the city center is covered by parks. As you walk through it, you can tell; it feels very open, very green. This isn't New York, where you have to bundle your dog into an apartment all day and then take them to the one little park they can play in. The city is incredibly walkable, and having a dog in many ways is the best way to explore it."

Scotland's compact capital is renowned for its gothic architecture, rolling hills, hidden laneways, and years upon years of history. But don't let the cathedral spires and gray skies give you the impression of austerity and stuffiness. A staple feature of Edinburgh's culture is its dog-friendliness.

Visitors accustomed to outside seating only for their pets are surprised by the fact that Edinburgh's charming pubs, vintage bars, and upscale restaurants allow well-behaved dogs inside as the norm. "It's hard to pick a particularly dog-friendly place to visit, because being dog-friendly isn't something that's necessarily advertised," Gareth reflected. "It's considered normal. Many places you can simply turn up with your dog, ask, and chances are they'll be happy to have you. Sometimes it's joked that it's easier to take a dog around Edinburgh than it is to take a child. Licensing laws restrict entry for under-eighteens in pubs, for example. But your dog can come right in."

Around the famous Royal Mile—the gothic cobblestoned tourist district of Edinburgh's Old Town, which houses Saint Giles' Cathedral and Edinburgh Castle—the staff at the Holyrood 9A pub are known to bring guest canines a bowl of water without the human even having to ask. Southwest from the Old Town toward the Meadows, other favorites include Blackbird Bar, with its impressive cocktails, and Piecebox Café, whose staff will often bring your dog a complimentary sausage. "One restaurant I enjoy in particular is called the City Cafe—to say they are dog-friendly undersells them in a way," Gareth explained. "They aren't a dog-themed café; they're fashioned after a diner. But you walk in with a dog and the staff are keen to bring them water and make friends. I joke sometimes that customers with dogs seem to get better attention, because the staff wants to gravitate toward them and say hello to the pup.

"Another place visitors should be sure to check out is a community hub called Summerhall. It's in an old veterinarian school, so it has that animal connection. It's a gin distillery, a brewery, and a festival performance space. They have a regular cinema night. It has a really lively, contemporary feel, a departure from the dark, quiet, old-fashioned pubs you often encounter. If you want to see a more modern side of Edinburgh with your dog, Summerhall is a wonderful place to visit."

Pet shops have been popping up in Edinburgh over the years, meeting a cultural need to treat your pet and give them the best of the best. "It's become a real lifestyle here," reflected Gareth. "If you're visiting you should check out Hill Lord. It's Edinburgh's oldest pet shop, now run by two brothers. It's a small little shop, a bit dark and old-fashioned. But they really know their customers, and they always enjoy making a fuss over your dog."

When it's time for a proper walk, you're never far from a green space in Edinburgh. The city's most famous park, Holyrood, is a 640-acre landscape of rolling green hills, trails and ponds in the middle of downtown. At certain points it can be hard to remember you're in a city, and haven't been teleported into the highlands. The highest point in the park is known as Arthur's Seat, and demarcates the tallest point of the extinct volcanoes that make up Edinburgh. Start from the bottom at the Palace of Holyroodhouse and wind your way to the top for a demanding stroll; you'll be rewarded with a windy, 360-degree bird's-eye view of the city and the ocean.

"Besides Holyrood, another favorite walk of mine is to follow the trail along the Water of Leith," Gareth shared. "It's not so much a river, but a stream that runs twelve and a half miles from the hills, through the city's suburbs and neighborhoods, and goes all the way down to the port of Leith. You can do little sections of it, kind of like a hop-on/hop-off bus, and explore many of Edinburgh's neighborhoods along the way."

As you walk through the city, be sure to keep an eye out for some of Edinburgh's famous dog statues. "Edinburgh was actually called out for having more statues of dogs than it has of historical women," Gareth chuckled. "It's not a pleasant trend, but definitely speaks to the cultural legacy of dog appreciation." Perhaps the most celebrated of these statues, a memorial to a Skye terrier nicknamed Greyfriars Bobby, is in Greyfriars Kirk, a seventeenth-century cemetery. Legend says Greyfriars Bobby guarded his master's grave every day for fourteen years until he died himself in 1872. Other notable dog statues around town include one of Sir Walter Scott, Scotland's great ambassador who is memorialized with his dog Maida, a Pyrenean wolfdog/ Highland deerhound cross, at his feet; and one featuring the physicist James Clerk Maxwell, who was said to always work with a dog named Toby by his side (although the dog changed, the name never did).

After hitting the hills of the city, visitors can consider resting their legs at the Prestonfield House hotel. "It's really more of an estate than a hotel," described Gareth. "Your dog gets his own breakfast in the morning, his own towels. The hotel also does a famous and sophisticated afternoon tea. Pop into the room, and you can see people nibbling on exquisite tea sandwiches with their dogs lounging right next to them. It's interesting to be in such a high-status surrounding with your dog right there with you.

"When people first come to Edinburgh, they are often surprised by the scale," Gareth concluded. "It's very small and compact, and walking around it is the best way to explore it. Dogs give us a great excuse to be curious, be adventurous, to find the hidden lanes and alleyways, and see where they lead. If you come to Edinburgh, just follow your dog. The best places are the places he will probably be drawn to."

GARETH DAVIES founded Edinburgh Expert Walking Tours (edinburghexpert.com) in 2014 after training as a tour guide with Edinburgh Bus Tours, the city's premier bus tour operator, and working at Edinburgh Castle. He specializes in small-group, private, and customized Edinburgh tours to offer a more personal, informative experience. He is an adopted native of Edinburgh, and has lived in the city since 1998. Dogs are welcome on Edinburgh Expert Walking Tours, and Gareth's own canine co-guide, Monty the French bulldog, often comes along as well.

If You Go

▶ **Getting There:** Edinburgh Airport is served by most major carriers, especially Delta (800-221-1212; delta.com), or, if you're coming from Europe, Ryanair (+44 871 246 0002; ryanair.com).

▶ **Best Time to Visit:** Scotland skies see year-round rain, but spring and summer offer the best chances for sun and flowers in the parks.

▶ **Accommodations:** Prestonfield House can be booked at prestonfield.com or by calling +44 131 225 7800, and a list of other dog-friendly venues can be found at the City of Edinburgh Council tourism website, edinburgh.org.

▶ **Supplies:** The pet shop Hill-Lord & Co (+44 131 229 6655; hill-lord.co.uk) is southwest of Old Town in the Marchmont neighborhood.

DESTINATION

40

SINGAPORE

RECOMMENDED BY **Stephen Cranston**

Some places are inherently well suited to a happy dog—rolling hills, wide-open spaces, a dry, cooler climate.

Singapore is not one of *those* places. But thanks to the imagination of its human inhabitants—like Stephen Cranston—it's become an attractive destination for canines.

"Necessity is the mother of invention," Stephen began, "and to create a positive environment for Singaporean dogs, a number of dog-friendly facilities needed to be created. The weather is too hot and humid to be conducive for dogs to be exercising. The terrain is flat, and there are not many open spaces available to run your dogs. The number of dog owners has increased, especially in the aftermath of the COVID pandemic. The government has tried to respond to the needs of dog owners by creating more infrastructure in the shape of dog parks and dog runs. And market forces have acted to fill in around the edges. Singaporeans have a very entrepreneurial spirit."

Singapore, an island just off the southern tip of the Malay Peninsula, is simultaneously a city, a state, and a nation. Though smaller than the state of Rhode Island with a population of less than six million, Singapore is one of the most affluent nations in the world, with a gross domestic product of nearly $340 billion (as of this writing). Since its days as an outpost of the British empire and major trading center, Singapore has been a vibrant melting pot of cultures; today, its population is composed primarily of people of Chinese, Malay, Indian, and Eurasian descent. Though densely populated, almost half the island is given over to green space. The notion of dogs as pets is still relatively new in Singapore, but its popularity is growing.

"I'd say that initially, at least for some Singaporeans, dogs were a little bit for show," Stephen said. "But residents are becoming much more involved with their dogs. Many

OPPOSITE:
Singaporeans
are increasingly
embracing
dogs, including
"Singapore
Specials"
(shown here).

DESTINATION

41

181

are first-generation dog owners, and haven't had a lot of experience with dogs. Overall, the society is learning to relax around canines." A good example of these evolving attitudes is the treatment of the city-state's street dogs, mongrels that once were called "pariah dogs." "These weren't the sort of dogs people wanted to own," Stephen explained. "Many pre-ferred a pedigreed dog; there was perhaps some status to that. Then people from abroad starting adopting those dogs from the shelters. The dogs were soon rebranded as 'Singapore Specials'; no one calls them street dogs or pariah dogs anymore. People have become fans."

While the average café or restaurant in Singapore does not welcome dogs, a number of dog cafés have sprung up to serve both humans and canines. "Most will offer menus for both parties, and dogs are free to roam the premises off-leash," Stephen added. Ménage Café, for example, offers dog dishes like sous-vide Wagyu beef and a cheddar cheese beef ball; at I.N.U Cafe & Boutique, entrées for canines include salmon Wooflesburg. Hydrotherapy is also an essential element in the Singaporean dog regimen. "Water parks provide a place where your dogs can splash around with their friends," Stephen said. At Wag & Wild, Singapore's largest dog water park (with over nineteen thousand square feet of space), swimming provides low-impact exercise, stimulation through socialization with other dogs, and a cooling break from the heat.

It was the absence of hilly terrain and dog-friendly open spaces that inspired Stephen to take dog exercise to a new level. "When I landed in Singapore, I had a big rottweiler that I wanted to help keep fit," he recalled. "I'd take him to the dog park, but it wasn't really fitness. At one point, my dog was given some medicine that seemed similar to prescriptions I'd been given myself. I asked a vet friend if it was the same, and he said yes, it was adapted from human medicine. I had some background in exercise science, and I thought that it could be applied to dogs." That's how Barker & Pooch, a nonprofit fitness program for dogs, was born. Canine fitness trainers work one-on-one with dog clients in a variety of programs customized for the individual pet's needs, including swimming, strength, and conditioning (including treadmills) and senior dog fitness. "Dogs will come to us once or twice a week," Stephen continued. "Strength training helps dogs build muscles, which will discourage joint problems. I think exercise also helps with behavior problems, which, in many cases, can stem from pent-up energy."

How might an ideal doggy day unfold in Singapore? Stephen was happy to provide a schedule: "Begin at Barker & Pooch for a high-energy workout. Your dog will do their swim and gym. From there, head to a dog spa. In addition to grooming, some provide treatments like mud baths and a nice massage—yes, there are dog masseurs. When your pooch is absolutely relaxed, you can have lunch together at one of the dog cafés, so you can meet some locals. If you're feeling the need for a little more exercise, visit one of Singapore's dog runs—there's a nice one at East Coast Park, which is one of the island's nicest parks. You want to end the day with a cruise along the coast on an old-style sailing ship." Guests sailing on the *Royal Albatross* Sunset Sail and Dinner Cruise, billed as the world's first dog cruise, enjoy five-course meals (three for canine passengers) as the boat slowly sails along the shoreline. Dogs and their people eat together at a table. Dinner is topped off with a serving Singapore's first and favorite dog ice cream, Pawlato.

Humans, incidentally, get ice cream, too.

STEPHEN CRANSTON hails from Northern Ireland, and first landed in Singapore in 1993. A strength and conditioning coach specializing in martial arts conditioning, he eventually turned his knowledge toward canine strength and conditioning. In 2019, after spending eight years developing a methodology for dogs, Stephen opened Barker & Pooch (barkerpooch.dog) to provide conditioning services to Singapore's canine population. He's also the founder of the Academy of Canine Exercise Science. He lives in Singapore with his wife, Roslyn, and his rottweiler, Hanna.

If You Go

▶ **Getting There:** Singapore's largest airport, Changi, is served by a number of carriers, including Singapore Airlines (833-727-0118; singaporeair.com).
▶ **Best Time to Visit:** Singapore has a fairly consistent climate—hot and fairly humid—throughout the year.
▶ **Accommodations:** The Singapore Tourism Board (+65 6736 2000; visitsingapore .com) lists dog-friendly hotels.
▶ **Supplies:** Singapore has a number of stores catering to your dog's needs, including Pet Master (+65 6565 6866; petmaster.com.sg).

MADRID

RECOMMENDED BY **Caitlyn Nissim**

With about one dog for every eleven residents, Madrid is proud to be the most dog-friendly city in the country known as La Piel de Toro. "Spain in general is very dog-loving," began Caitlyn Nissim. "A lot of people have dogs, and it's normal for people to have dogs in apartments, and take them just about everywhere. They are a normal part of daily life. Madrid was the first city in Spain to allow dogs on the Metro, outside of commute hours. Everywhere with a terrace is dog-friendly in Spain, and nearly every place you visit has a terrace."

OPPOSITE:
Paella is beloved
by everyone in
Madrid.

The sweltering summer heat has inspired Madrid's ever-growing rooftop bar scene, allowing visitors to gaze at panoramic views of the city's historic architectural skyline in impeccably posh settings, with a glass of sangria in hand. In the wintertime, however, the cold has a way of sending all mammals indoors, and visitors can find refuge in several delightful indoor cafés. Some dog-welcoming local favorites include Zenith, with its all-day breakfast and happy hour, and the famously photogenic brunch café EatMyTrip. When visitors walk into the chain's Madrid location, they are greeted with the motto "I want it all" emblazoned on the back wall, before tucking into meals of unrivaled creativity, such as multicolored cakes that resemble flowery still lifes, cotton candy–topped pancakes, and eggs scrambled with kimchi and marinated salmon. "You want take a picture of everything," reflected Caitlyn. "And the best part is, they are dog-friendly inside.

"My favorite restaurant, though, is probably El Perro y la Galleta," Caitlyn continued. "The inside is all dog-themed, and decorated in this kind of gilded vintage style. That was Remy's first European café. He was very curious, very excited. They let dogs sit with you right at the table, and the staff is so warm and welcoming. They have dog portraits everywhere. The location closest to Retiro Park is a favorite."

Madrid is famous for its elegant and lush city parks, but most consider El Retiro, with its 125 hectares of open space and fifteen thousand trees, the champion of them all. There are special agility areas for dogs, along with dedicated drinking fountains. The civic service group Community of Madrid provides free wag bags on the sides of waste bins, just in case you left yours at the hotel. Visitors can lounge on one of the park's many benches and watch the rowboats drift by on the sparkling lake, or stroll around the grounds and take in the various statues and monuments. Whatever your religious inclinations, be sure not to miss *El Ángel Caído* (*The Fallen Angel*), the world's only sculpture dedicated to the devil—which sits almost precisely 666 meters above sea level. Also consider popping into the French-style garden known as the Parterre, which holds one of Madrid's oldest trees, a two-hundred-year-old Montezuma cypress nicknamed "El Abuelo" ("The Grandfather"). Although dogs are not allowed inside Retiro Park's famous Palacio de Cristal (Glass Castle), which is often reserved for museum displays, the 1887 house of wrought iron and glass is a not-to-miss wonder for architecture buffs. "The first time we arrived in Madrid with Remy back in March 2020, right before the pandemic began," Caitlyn rememberd, "we were in Retiro Park, and I was so worried after fourteen hours of travel, how he was going to do with jet lag and the new environment. But he was thrilled. To this day, he loves Retiro Park so much."

Though Madrid is an immense city, getting around is quite easy. "Generally speaking, you'll want to try and stay in the city center," reflected Caitlyn. "Everything is very walkable from there. But if you want to go to a museum or a play at Teatro de Títeres, be sure you're in a hotel or Airbnb that allows dogs to be alone for a bit of time. It's quite common, but it's still something you want to double-check before you book."

The fact that that all dogs are allowed on the Metro system, as mentioned earlier, greatly facilitates your travel around Madrid. So long as your dog is on a short leash and under voice control, they are welcome on the Metro. "Muzzles are required at the owner's discretion. It's better to have one if you know your dog is still training or gets nervous around crowds," cautioned Caitlyn, "But again, the fact that the dogs are allowed at all is really unique for Spain."

If you prefer to travel solo, you can always opt for a taxi. "Dogs are generally welcome in taxis," Caitlyn said. "We've never had a problem, but it's always best to ask the driver before you get in. You can also hail a ride with Cabify, which is an app service, and dogs are welcome so long as they are in a carrier.

"We were easily able to find dog-friendly hotels, and affordable ones, too," continued Caitlyn. "My favorite is probably the Petit Palace. There are several around Madrid and throughout Spain, and they are all so dog-friendly. They provided a bed, a little bag of food, even, and bowls. Many hotels in Spain enforce a pet fee, but they do not. And the whole staff just loved on Remy.

"My favorite thing about Madrid," Caitlyn concluded, "is that every time I go there, I discover something new to do, something I haven't seen or explored yet. It will always be a really special place for me."

CAITLYN NISSIM is the founder of the @remyaroundtheworld Instagram channel, sharing dog-friendly travel adventures, tips, and advice for over twenty European cities, from London to the Amalfi Coast. By empowering pet parents with practical tips about pet passports, airport relief areas, public transportation requirements, and, of course, dog-friendly beaches, restaurants, shops, and parks, Caitlyn aims to increase responsible pet travel so both humans and dogs can enjoy their vacations abroad. After meeting Remy in Texas, Caitlyn relocated the two of them to Spain, where she currently lives with her husband.

If You Go

▶ **Getting There:** Madrid-Barajas Airport is served by several international carriers, and is the hub of Iberia (800-772-4642; iberia.com) and Air Europa (844-415-3955; aireuropa .com).

▶ **Best Time to Visit:** Fall or spring tend to be favorite times, when balmy winds blow through the city. January 17 marks the festival of San Antón, the patron saint of animals— you can visit the Church of San Antón in Madrid to have your pet blessed with holy water.

▶ **Accommodations:** The Petit Palace (petitpalace.com) is a small chain of hotels with many locations throughout Spain.

▶ **Supplies:** Petmanía (+34 914 34 59 21) is a wonderful supplier close to Retiro Park.

DESTINATION

42

LES QUATRE VALLÉES

RECOMMENDED BY **Kristel Segeren**

In the Swiss Alps, winter skiers revel in fresh powder, gorgeous runs, and plush après-ski accommodations, and summer hikers meander through meadows of wildflowers that seem pulled straight out of a fairy tale. "Whether the snow is crackling under the paws, the alpine fields are in full bloom, you're chilling by an alpine lake, or smelling fresh autumn leaves on the wooded slopes—the Swiss Alps have this high *jodelahiti* feeling all year round," described Kristel Segeren. "Life is pretty peaceful this many meters above sea level. I think mountains have a way of relativizing things; they just humble us with their perspectives. We have always brought along our dog when we come out here, and many other outdoorsy people do the same. And why wouldn't we? This place is just perfect for dogs that love to explore, and they are fully welcomed just about everywhere."

Les Quatre Vallées is one of the biggest ski regions in Switzerland, comprising a cluster of charming alpine villages that are interconnected by dog-friendly year-round ski lifts and hiking trails. "Many of the chairs can close up, so that you can safely include your dog for the ride," said Kristel. "The village of Haute-Nendaz is the place where we always stay, which is a bit of a family village, located close to Mont Fort. We like Haute-Nendaz because the town, at over four thousand feet altitude, makes a wonderful base for hiking, especially day hikes. Nearby you can also find more upscale Verbier, the low-key village of La Tzoumaz, and the more commercial Veysonnaz—all easy to reach. Whatever place you pick, the ski lift is a perfect means of transportation to explore the area, and you can bring your dog with you—no need to pay extra."

Other notable trails include the valley of Evolène, about a half-hour drive from Haute-Nendaz, a glacier-side path that meanders along in the shadow of the Dent Blanche; or the flat road to Lac de Derborence, Europe's youngest natural lake, recently created by a

OPPOSITE:
Fields of flowers in the Swiss Alps make for happy romping.

DESTINATION

43

landslide. "Another cool hike is right above Verbier, along the Col des Mines," Kristel described. "This is a drop-dead gorgeous setting, especially in autumn, with all the different-colored leaves in front of the snowcapped peaks in the back. During the hikes you might see some wildlife, and lots of alpine cows equipped with those giant melodic bells. Chapo always finds entertainment in the squirrels and marmots. But don't pity them—they are way quicker and smarter than our little goof."

Although the Alps are known for their steep slopes, there are plenty of flat trails to be found as well. Some favorite routes include Les Bisses, a network of historic irrigation channels that runs through the forests along the valleys. "The Bisse du Milieu, Grand Bisse de Vex, and Bisse de Saxon are our favorites," continued Kristel. "These pathways are well-defined along the slopes, but there's also shade and water, which our dog appreciates greatly during the hotter days, and from time to time you run into a cute café along the road, which the humans appreciate during the hotter days. Since the bisses are so well connected, you could easily make a multiday trail out of it and stay every night in another village.

"If you prefer to unplug even more, it's possible to do hut-to-hut hikes. But mind that some of these high-altitude trails can be technical [difficult] and not suitable for all dogs. What I love about the slightly lower fields is that every April and May, they are brightly blooming. There's a rainbow of color on display. The sight of waterfalls in the back. You sometimes feel like Julie Andrews—singing 'The Hills Are Alive.' It's too perfect."

While summer offers green hills, fairy-tale wildflowers, and sprightly animal encounters, winter is also a brilliant time to visit. "I also have seen people bring their dogs while skiing." Kristel continued. "You ski down, and your dog runs along with you down the side. That's not for all dogs, of course, but it's extremely fun if your dog likes the snow and you've trained them to keep up with you."

Beyond its spectacular natural beauty, there are other reasons to visit Switzerland in winter (or really, anytime) with your dog. "One word: cheese," laughed Kristel. "I don't know about your dog, but mine would absolutely do anything for a piece. The smell of raclette, cheesy fondue, or Gruyère is never far away over here. Sitting in front of the fire with your dog in your chalet at the end of the day, eating some raclette to regain your strength after a long hike along the slopes—that sounds about right, doesn't it?"

Many charming cafés and restaurants dot the slopes of the Alps, and it is normal to bring your dog along for an après-ski fondue or a post-hike bratwurst. "My favorite place is Maison de la Fôret in La Tzoumaz, which is next to the Bisse de Saxon," Kristel added.

"It's a cute and easygoing café, with local dishes, picnic tables, and a small museum about the area. Indie kind of bands come here as well to play from time to time. Another nice joint close to the Bisse de Saxon is the Cabane Balavaux. Dogs are welcome on the terrace here, which has a bit of a Himalaya-like feel and offers gorgeous views on the area.

"In general, the people who live in the Alps are quite open to dogs. Chapo has been welcomed everywhere so far. I guess that's just the culture up here," Kristel concluded. "Of course, I wouldn't bring my dog to a museum in Geneva, but up here, dogs seem part of the outdoor lifestyle."

KRISTEL SEGEREN worked as an editor and photographer in Costa Rica, where she adopted her dog, Chapo, from the streets. After a couple of years living on the Caribbean shores and traveling all over the Americas, she returned home to the Netherlands from this tropical adventure, showing her dog the very best Europe has to offer. Although Chapo is a three-legged dog, she is always wildly excited to go on a new hiking adventure. From tropical heat to icy snow conditions—she can withstand it all, and luckily for her, squirrels can be chased around the world. Follow them along the way on thetinytravelogue.com.

If You Go

▶ **Getting There:** The closest airport is Geneva, which is a hub for Swiss Airlines (833-626-0737; swiss.com). From the airport, it's best to rent a car to get into the Quatre Vallées area, rather than taking a train.

▶ **Best Time to Visit:** The Swiss Alps welcome vacationers all year, depending on your preferred activity. Hiking is best July through August, and January through February see the deepest snow for winter sports.

▶ **Accommodations:** Many hotels are pet-friendly, but most travelers find it nicer to rent their own chalet, which are available through a number of agencies.

▶ **Supplies:** Petfriends in Sion (+41 061 568 99 11; petfriends.ch) serves the area with a large array of goods.

NASHVILLE

RECOMMENDED BY **Lauren Hays**

"During 2020 when everyone was stuck inside and thinking about adopting a dog, my husband and I decided to adopt one, too," Lauren Hays recalled. "It seemed like the perfect time. So we went to Wags and Walks Nashville, and we adopted Dottie. After two or three days, she was acting kind of weird, and we weren't sure what was going on. Finally, on the fifth day, we took her to the vet and found out she was pregnant! She gave birth to three puppies that night.

"After that whole experience, we noticed she had some anxiety and stress being left alone. I went looking for some restaurants and dog-friendly shops and I discovered it was harder to find everything I wanted at once. So, in turn, I decided to create @dogfriend lynash. Nashville has so many dog owners, and this is overall a very dog-friendly city, so why not show it off?" Lauren continued.

Nashville's tourism has spent the past decade skyrocketing, with no end in sight. A discerning whiskey and craft beer scene caters to aficionados, and foodies can savor legendary Tennessee-style Southern cuisine (be sure to try the catfish, a plate of meat and three, and, of course, hot chicken). "It's a destination city, but also very fun to live in," commented Lauren. "There are always so many things to do." On balmy summer nights, when the music is hopping and the streets are surging with life, the pups can come out and enjoy the party, too.

"The first time we went out with Dottie, we took her to a tiki bar," Lauren continued. "And I have never seen her happier to be out with us. She was smiling like a human being. One of the bartenders was making our drinks and brought them over, and while Dottie is normally pretty shy, she could not keep her eyes off this bartender. It felt like we had a child who had a crush on the waiter. He eventually came over and gave her some

OPPOSITE:
Nashville's
vibrant, bustling
downtown has
many happy stops
for dogs to enjoy.

treats and some pets, and I have never seen a dog give such honest puppy eyes. I love having that be our first memory of her going out on the town with us and also our very first dog-friendly post."

Many Nashville eateries have a spacious patio, and dogs are welcome guests. However, what makes Nashville unique is the exceptional number of venues that welcome dogs inside. This is especially good news if you choose to avoid the brutal heat of summer and visit during the tamer spring, fall, or even winter season. Some favorites include Pins Mechanical Company, a game-themed bar where humans can play games like duckpin bowling and bocce. The vintage, wood-paneled Americano Lounge serves up craft cocktails and elegant coffee drinks, and your dog can join you at the table. "A favorite place of mine is called Red Bicycle Coffee," added Lauren. "You can hang out, get cozy inside, and chill with your dog. They even have their own Instagram page called Pups of Red Bicycle that shows the doggos coming in, getting a pup cup, and just hanging with their humans. Another indoor favorite of mine is Diskin Cider. They are incredible, and of course, the cider is delicious. Huge seating, board games—it's great for groups. They just got their own little golden retriever who is always in there, too."

The hospitality doesn't halt at mealtime. Nashville is an enormously walkable city, and most of the interesting attractions you'll see about town don't require you to park your dog on the curb. "I think you can kind of tell a dog-friendly city by if they are going to let your dog inside most places around town," Lauren observed. "In Nashville, it's kind of assumed you can, unless you see a sign that says you can't, kind of like Nashville parking. There are a lot of small businesses, and most of those owners—if they don't have a shop dog themselves—are willing to let your dog come in with you!"

An especially dog-friendly neighborhood to explore is the iconic Germantown. Named for the immigrants who settled in Nashville in the 1800s, Germantown has earned itself a spot on the National Register of Historic Places. It plays home to Bicentennial Capitol Mall State Park, a majestic landscape of patriotic memorials, stone columns, and cool fountains. Autumn brings radiant displays of color along the tree-lined avenues and manicured lawns. The upscale neighborhood also contains many of Nashville's most delightful restaurants, such as Picca Pollo a la Brasa and Von Elrod's Beer Hall & Kitchen, as well as plenty of boutiques. "Virtually every small business over in Germantown is dog-friendly," Lauren added. "Of course, you always want to be polite and ask the owner, but in my experience, they almost always encourage it."

Pet-friendly is more the norm at Nashville hotels than the exception. And if you ever need to pop in out of the rain or take a breather from the humidity, the city's glamorous hotel lobbies are extremely hospitable to dogs and humans alike. "Most people think you have to be staying in a hotel to go inside," Lauren observed. "But that's not always true! Nashville hotels have these amazing lobbies with cafés and lovely seating where you can go in with your dog, have a coffee, maybe a little meal, and cowork all day with your fur baby! Many times, the attendees will even come over with a treat for your dog. Our favorite is probably the Graduate Hotel. But it's the same with another of our favorites, the W located in the Gulch, another walkable area with a little hidden dog park too. These hotels will go above and beyond to make your dog feel like a special guest."

LAUREN HAYS is the founder of Dog-Friendly Nashville (@dogfriendlynash), providing Nashville guests and locals with countless answers to the question "Where can I bring my dog?" The goal of @dogfriendlynash is to bring ease and fun to pet owners whether they're just visiting or living in Music City! From dog-friendly patios, markets, shops, events, meetups, and more; we hope to provide an easy go-to platform where anyone can scroll to find the perfect ways to spend their day(s) with their pup by their side! Along with this, it's been a great platform for sharing local shelters who are in need of donations, fosters, or adoptions, and spread the word to the incredible dog community.

If You Go

▶ **Getting There:** Nashville International Airport is served by several carriers, especially Southwest (800-435-9792; southwest.com).

▶ **Best Time to Visit:** Nashville has something for every season: spring flowers, summer festivals, autumn colors, and wonderful winter Christmas decorations.

▶ **Accommodations:** The Graduate Nashville (615-551-2700; graduatehotels.com/nashville) is a pet-friendly hotel (the Graduate Hotels brand has locations around the country). Vacation rentals also tend to be dog-friendly; just double-check at booking.

▶ **Supplies:** Nashville Pet Products (615-242-2223; nashvillepetproducts.com) is a particular favorite. Be sure to say hello to the two store cats.

AUSTIN

RECOMMENDED BY **Edward Flores**

"I come from a really small border town on the southern tip of Texas," Edward Flores began, "and dogs are not family there. They are property. They are either your baby and live on your lap, or are outside tied to a tree and never come in the house. Austin dog culture is very different from that. I've been working with dogs for about fifteen years, and when I came to Austin for the first time, it was a shock. Dogs weren't treated like they were disposable or tied up outside. They were family. It was such a beautiful thing to see, all these animals able to be on patios with their owners, and come into department stores. Austin is one of the most exhilarating, dog-friendly cities in the world."

OPPOSITE:
A husky takes
in the view of
downtown
Austin from
Lady Bird Lake.

Sometimes called Bat City and the "Live Music Capital of the World," and ever striving to stay weird, Austin is a city that draws tourists from all over the globe. As its base of tech workers, left-leaning politicos, and gourmet foodies increases, so has its love for man's best friend. "Austin is the largest no-kill city in the nation," Edward continued. "Our shelters are often observed and dissected by other cities trying to put similar policies in place; they come here to learn how we make it work. In my opinion, a lot of it is the community and the culture. There's a huge base of people ready to shelter, foster, volunteer, and donate to the cause of keeping dogs alive. Keeping dogs healthy and happy is a passion project for everyone. It's almost a little bit of a joke—just about everyone has a rescue. If you have a purebred, you might get heckled a little."

The city's dog offerings include countless boarding day cares, grooming salons, training centers, and dog-friendly bars and restaurants. "It seems like every apartment has a self-service dog wash station and a small dog park," Edward said. "A huge part of my business is visiting 'yappy hours' at housing complexes, because almost everyone has a dog. And there are tons of off-leash parks, too many to even count off the top of my head. One

DESTINATION

45

of my favorite spots to take Kaxan, our rescue, is Zilker Metropolitan Park. It's a massive off-leash dog run, and it's not fenced in, so, you need to be confident in your dog's off-leash skills. It's where Austin City Limits is held. Kaxan and I love to wake up before the sunrise and head there. At that time, you just about have the whole place to yourself, and can watch the sunrise over the city skyline. Kaxan loves it, he runs like crazy. Be sure to bring a towel for morning dew on the paws."

Most restaurants in Austin begin as food trucks, clustering in dog-friendly open-air courts where diners can enjoy a meal with their pup beside them. Increasingly, the trucks are featuring dog-friendly menus, serving up sausages, hot dogs, and house-made treats. You can also seek out the Original Dog Treat Truck Co. and have your order of Woof Waffles delivered by Lily, the company's star-employee golden retriever. "A favorite dining spot of Kaxan's is Yard Bar, which is both a dog bar and a dog park. They have a restaurant attached to it with a menu for humans and a menu for dogs, so you can share a little meal together on the patio.

"Something I recently saw that blew me away," Edward chuckled, "was at place called Paws on Chicon, a pet boutique now on their second location. They just brought in a fro-yo machine. Just like the kind you see at Dairy Queen, except it's for the dogs. They lay out a topping bar, the flavors rotate. It was incredible. That's another thing about Austin," he continued. "The small business owners that make up most of the dog industry here, we all know each other, we all help each other and give back. There are enough dogs to go around that no one ever gets competitive, and the industry is more communal."

One of the largest communal activities that takes place is Barks for Beers, an event that helps fundraise for Divine Canines. About one hundred breweries in the city participate. "People pay thirty dollars for a pint glass," described Edward, "and they get to go to any of the participating breweries and get a free pour. And all of these breweries are dog-friendly. The dogs can come with you inside, and there are dog treats at every counter. The breweries in Austin are generally very welcoming to dog owners, because they know who their clients are. And a lot of them are using scraps and things that might otherwise be wasted, and turning them into these gourmet, in-house dog treats. It's a win for everybody."

If you're only in town for a few days, consider splurging on a room at the Westin Austin Downtown, where guest canines are given a small robe, a bed, a special patio, and, of course, complimentary treats. If you have more than a few days, consider driving outside the city limits to visit a dog ranch, such as A to Z Dog Ranch or Oeste. "These places are popping up outside the city, where you can glamp with your dog," Edward said. "You can get a doggy tipi and have doggy s'mores. They really are quite lovely."

A particularly fun time to visit is during the Mighty Texas Dog Walk, which typically takes place in March. The event is put on by Service Dogs, Inc., which helps provide trained service dogs to those in need. "It takes over thirty thousand dollars to train a service dog," Edward noted, "and the crazy thing is, ninety percent of these dogs are pulled from shelters. These are dogs that were thrown away as strays and end up helping people. At Mighty Texas Dog Walk, all the dogs get numbers and bibs, and walk the mile. From a distance, you just see this wave of dogs walking down from the state capital—it's huge. The first time I went, that was the moment I really knew I loved this city, and this is where I wanted to live, to be around the passion that every single dog owner has for their animal. It's contagious.

"At the end of the walk, everyone gets a little medal and then it turns into this incredible festival. You've got Petco and PetSmart, and the small businesses, and even the local grocery stores. People walk away with armfuls of bags of treats and samples. It's dog swag-bag heaven.

"Austin has been changing a lot lately, growing quickly," Edward reflected. "Some people get cranky about it. But I love it, I love the way that it's growing. If you come to Austin, get ready— you're going to experience something really special with your dog."

EDWARD FLORES is the trainer of the *KXAN News* mascot, Kaxan, and producer on *CityDog Austin*. In 2008, after a career as a bank manager, he become a partner in Mud Puppies, Austin's premier playcare, boarding, grooming, and training center. Edward is also a proud board member for Austin Dog Rescue, and has been serving as a foster parent since 2009. Edward's commitment to excellence in business and community service is evident by his numerous achievements. He has been a member of the City of Austin's Animal Advisory Commission (appointed by Jimmy Flanagan) since 2017, a member of the City of Austin Off Leash Area Advisory Committee from 2011–2012, and a therapy dog team member with Divine Canines since 2014. In 2019, Kaxan, a rescue dog who was found abandoned behind his eponymous TV station, was named one of the top three therapy dogs in the nation by the American Humane Hero Dog Awards.

DESTINATION

45

If You Go

▶ **Getting There:** Austin-Bergstrom International Airport is served by a number of carriers, especially American (800-433-7300; aa.com) and Southwest (800-435-9792; southwest.com).

▶ **Best Time to Visit:** To avoid the sweltering summer heat, aim for autumn or spring. The Mighty Texas Dog Walk is typically held in March.

▶ **Accommodations:** The Westin Austin Downtown (512-391-2333; marriott.com) asks that you mention your pet at booking. Visit Austin also lists a number of dog-friendly accommodations at austintexas.org.

▶ **Supplies:** Austin has a large number of pet stores, a perennial favorite being Paws on Chicon (512-273-7297; pawsonchicon.com).

DESTINATION

45

BANGKOK

RECOMMENDED BY **Patrick Flood**

The "land of smiles" is no stranger to visitors in search of a much-needed tropical vacation. Thailand is famous for its *sabai sabai* hospitality and coastline of nearly endless white sand beaches, warm turquoise water, and swaying palm trees. "I came to Thailand five years ago," began Patrick Flood. "I wanted to take a little break from my work back home. I thought maybe I'd be here for six months. That turned into five years and counting."

A Buddhist country with strong undercurrents of Hinduism and Chinese Taoism, Thailand's spiritual and philosophical heritage come together to create a deeply welcoming environment to all animals—including canines. "The dog culture has gotten stronger in the last five years," Patrick continued. "People have always had dogs, but they are traditionally outdoor pets, and thought of more as outdoor guards rather than members of the indoor family. And of course, there are a lot of stray dogs, which everyone is cautious of. At the same time, there's a strong culture of people taking care of those strays, leaving them rice and chicken, respecting their neighborhoods, things like that. The dogs we adopted were actually strays. There was a litter of puppies living in a construction site, and every day I passed them on my way to work. First there were six, then four . . . after a while, there were only two. They were well fed by the neighborhood, but they had fleas and some other health issues. We thought either they would be strays their whole (short) life, or we should take them home. So we took them home."

The Bangkok skyline is packed with skyscrapers. Nearly eleven million people in cars and tuk-tuks and on foot rush back and forth through the streets. But dedicated parks—many specifically designed for dogs—do exist in the green metropolis. "During

DESTINATION

46

the pandemic, more and more people wanted a companion," Patrick said. "And the need for places to go with that companion has risen." Today, there is an ever-increasing number of green "dog-running" spaces—beautiful fenced parks and cafés where dogs can stretch their legs in safe and welcoming company. "You can have a coffee, chat with other people who love their dog as much as you love yours, and your dog can actually run and play with other dogs without you having to worry," Patrick added. As your pup gets a few laps in, be sure to try some of the local favorite coffee drinks. "I'm a big fan of orange juice and coffee," enthused Patrick. "It's called a black and orange, and it's delicious. I waited way too long to try it. There are also coconut water and coffee, or an Americano with honey and lemon, which is like an Arnold Palmer but with a lighter roast coffee. It's so addicting, especially on a hot day. I mean, iced coffee and your dog—what more could you ask for?"

Some favorites green spaces in downtown Bangkok include Paws and Pals, a modern café with a fenced green lawn for dogs to run free, and Trail and Tail, a café, park, pet hotel, and all-around dog-friendly microuniverse set up by the city. "Trail and Tail was one of the first places designed for the dog community to exercise and socialize their pets, and it's still one of the most popular," described Patrick. Also consider stopping by Mega Park at Mega Bangna, a seven-zoned modern indoor/outdoor shopping mall built with dogs in mind (there's even a pet gym). Each zone has an individual theme, while the surrounding mall includes green runs, decorative gardens, nature walks, and an elevated skywalk. "Because it's so hot here, shopping malls are huge, and this led to the trend of dog-friendly shopping malls," Patrick explained. "The malls provide wag bags and wipes. It's tailored to smaller dogs—most pet dogs in Thailand are of that smaller lapdog variety—but they don't discriminate."

Visitors should be advised that although many cafés are pet-friendly, more formal restaurants in Thailand do not allow dogs inside. "Mostly you'll be on the patio," noted Patrick. "There are a lot of places that are still not pet-friendly—but the staff will always work with you to find a solution. Thai people are very accommodating, and hospitality is valued."

Visitors can happily spend all their time in Bangkok, but the smaller towns and gorgeous islands outside the city are well worth exploring with your dog in tow. "A lot of people, especially European vacationers, take weekend trips from Bangkok out to Pattaya," Patrick observed. "It's about a two-hour drive southeast, and right on the ocean." On the

DESTINATION

46

Bay of Bangkok, the resort town Hua Hin is perfect for those looking for a calmer vacation not too far from the metropolis. "Hua Hin is easier to get to than an island, because it doesn't involve a ferry," reflected Patrick. "It could be the most dog-friendly town in Thailand. It's a lovely small seaside community, with beautiful beaches and several pet-friendly hotels."

If you have time, consider a trip to Thailand's southern coast for a visit to Phuket. Thailand's largest island is famous for its jewel-toned coastlines and surreal, rocky skyline. A quick flight from Bangkok is the easiest way to arrive, although an overnight bus can make the trip. "Unlike Bangkok, it's very green, a real-life island paradise," added Patrick. "It's very dog-friendly. You can stay in a five-star villa or a little twenty-dollars-a-night bungalow, and your dog will usually be welcome.

"When we first adopted our stray dogs, we were nervous. But ultimately, dogs are a great stress-reliever, and everyone seems to feel that, especially during the pandemic. Now that we have the dogs, we've noticed that whenever we walk anywhere, people talk to us who normally wouldn't. They say hello, pet the dog, share their own dog stories. In a way, dogs allow you to meet people that you never would've met, especially if you aren't native and people might be wary to come up to you. But the presence of a pet dog seems to let people drop their guard and want to say hello."

PATRICK FLOOD is the cofounder of Pet Friendly Thailand, the largest and most user-friendly online resource for both English- and Thai-speaking pet owners living in or traveling to Thailand. Through the website and social media channels, Patrick seeks to connect pet families with thousands of pet-friendly hotels, parks, pools, events, and cafés throughout the country.

If You Go

▶ **Getting There:** Suvarnabhumi Airport is served by most international carriers and is the hub of Thai Airways (+66 2356 1111; thaiairways.com). Bangkok Airways (+66 2270 6699; bangkokair.com) runs frequent flights between the capital and other destinations in Thailand, including Phuket.

▶ **Best Time to Visit:** December through March is the main tourist season and has the clearest weather. Monsoon rains tend to drench from July to October.

▶ **Accommodations:** Pet Friendly Thailand (petfriendlythailand.com) list a number of hotels throughout the country. The Tourism Authority of Thailand also lists reliable accommodations at tourismthailand.org.

▶ **Supplies:** Bangkok has a number of pet stores, but visitors can also check out Chatuchak Weekend Market—Southeast Asia's largest outdoor market, with more than fifteen thousand stalls—which has a huge section just for pets.

KANAB

RECOMMENDED BY **Paul Gagner**

The brilliant sandstone cliffs, vertiginous slot canyons, and vast sagebrush plains around Kanab, Utah, are as Wild West as one could hope for. It's no wonder, then, that so many westerns—including *Gunsmoke*, *How the West Was Won*, and *The Outlaw Josey Wales*—have been filmed here (accordingly, Kanab has dubbed itself "Little Hollywood"). Many people visit to experience the grandeur of southern Utah's rock-hewn attractions. And thanks in part to a man-made local institution, many bring (or meet!) their dogs here.

"Kanab is right in the middle of the Grand Circle, which refers to the radius of famous sites in the region," Paul Gagner observed. "We're thirty-five minutes from the eastern gate of Zion National Park, an hour and fifteen minutes from Lake Powell, an hour and a half from Bryce Canyon National Park, and an hour and forty-five minutes from the North Rim of the Grand Canyon. We have access to a wide variety of natural phenomena for people to experience—rock formations, slot canyons, Native American rock art, dinosaur footprints. As outdoor guides, my wife and I travel around the area a good deal. Every time we check off one item on our 'must-see' list, it seems we add seven more. There are the national parks and other more publicized spots that folks read about, but there are also many 'locals-only' spots that are equally spectacular that most visitors don't know about. That's where we come into play."

Dreamland Safari Tours leads a number of different adventures around southern Utah, and dogs are welcome on most. "We cater to whatever our visitors' ability levels and interests are," Paul continued, "and how much time they have. For travelers with less mobility, we can do driving/sightseeing trips; we can also do ten-plus-mile hiking days, and everything in between. Some trips are three hours; others are all-day, over-

OPPOSITE:
Dogs are invited to join guides on tours of the geologic wonders around Kanab; here, Dreamland Safari's staff dog Dasher and guide Andrea Jasper explore the Wave in Vermilion Cliffs National Monument.

night, or multiday. Sometimes people will book a private tour and take their dog along. Other times, someone will book a spot or two on a public tour and ask if they can bring their dog. Before we accept a reservation, we'll make sure that anyone else signed up for that particular tour is okay with a dog. If people are booking a private tour and are not traveling with their dog but would *like* a dog along, we can make our husky, Dasher, available."

Paul shared a few of the most popular tours Dreamland leads: "One of our favorite all-day tours is to White Pocket, which is in the Vermilion Cliffs National Monument in northern Arizona. It's an absolutely stunning rock formation, with multicolor striations of white, yellow, red, orange, and pink, plus bulges that look like mushrooms or brains. It's a long day—nine hours, with a two-and-a-half-hour drive each way. But if you're coming to southern Utah, it's not something to miss."

Southern Utah is known for its slot canyons, narrow gorges that have been formed from water coursing through the region's sedimentary deposits. "The Peek-a-Boo tour is a great introduction to slot canyons," Paul described, "and is a shorter tour, at three hours. I should point out that there are three Peek-a-Boo Canyons in Utah—one near Bryce, one near the town of Escalante, and ours, which is just north of Kanab. It's a tough drive in there through deep sand; you need a four-wheel-drive vehicle with good clearance to get in and out. The red rock canyon itself is a half mile long, and a fairly easy walk. The walls climb eighty feet; about halfway through, there are steps that were carved by the Ancestral Pueblo people almost a thousand years ago. The hike up Peek-a-Boo Canyon can be combined with a few side trips. One brings visitors to a spot in the White Cliffs area of Grand Staircase called the White Wave, where there's a petroglyph panel that was created by the Ancestral Pueblo people. Another combines Peek-a-Boo with a stop at a place we call Dinosaur Trackside, where there are hundreds of dinosaur tracks. This is a favorite with kids. Another favorite for folks who are looking for a slightly mellower experience is the Sunset Safari, which combines a visit to Peek-a-Boo with a stop at Red Knoll to watch the sun set over the eastern cliffs of Zion National Park."

The tours Paul mentioned are all popular with guests traveling with their dogs. But he did offer a caveat: "The vehicle we use to get to the attractions is climate controlled. But outside conditions can be very hot in the summer, generally mid-June to mid-September. The air temperature might be close to one hundred degrees, and with heat radiating off the rocks and sand, it can be closer to one hundred twenty degrees. We don't recommend taking your dogs out in that kind of heat."

Once your desert exploration is done, a number of restaurants in Kanab have outdoor patios and are happy to host you and your dog. A few of Paul's favorites include Wild Thyme Cafe, Sego, Vermillion 45, and Escobar's.

As alluded to earlier, Kanab is home to a very special institution that's literally saved the lives of thousands of dogs and other animals: Best Friends Animal Society. Best Friends was founded in 1984 to provide a sanctuary for unwanted pets, housing and finding homes for them while promoting the notion of no-kill shelters. At the time Best Friends was founded, kill shelters were the norm; some seventeen million dogs and cats were euthanized annually in the US. Thanks in part to Best Friend's efforts, the number of animals killed annually in shelters has been reduced to under one million a year. Today, a third of counties/municipalities that offer animal shelter-ing services are no-kill. Best Friends can comfortably accommodate up to 1,600 dogs, cats, birds, bunnies, horses, pigs, and other animals; it's the largest sanctuary of its kind in the United States.

Visitors are welcome at Best Friends, with regular tours offered; volunteer opportuni-ties are also available. The Best Friends Roadhouse and Mercantile offers forty pet-centric hotel rooms, and perks that include pet-washing facilities and a pet park with splash water features.

PAUL GAGNER has spent more than four decades exploring, adventuring, and putting up first ascents on rock across the US and internationally. While Paul's first outdoor love was Yosemite, he is proud to call the Utah desert home, and is excited to be managing Dreamland Safari Tours (435-291-1060; dreamlandtours.net) together with his wife, Sunny. Beyond his adventurous outdoor pursuits, Paul brings long years of outdoor industry executive management experience to Dreamland Safari Tours. Prior to moving to Kanab, Paul led the outdoor division of Nite Ize after serving as president of Sierra Designs for several years. Back in the 1980s, Paul spent seven seasons as a climbing ranger in Grand Teton National Park, where he participated in upward of two hundred rescues and was among the first National Park Service employees to be certified for helicopter-rappel rescues. Paul's "can-do" attitude and unshakeable calm make him a favorite of guests and guides alike. Paul is a certified Wilderness First Responder.

If You Go

▶ **Getting There:** Las Vegas's Harry Reid International Airport is roughly two hundred miles away, and is served by most major carriers. Utah's St. George Regional Airport is eighty miles' distant, and is served by several carriers, including United (800-864-8331; united.com) and Delta (800-221-1212; delta.com).

▶ **Best Time to Visit:** Sunny skies are the norm most of the year, though summer can see high temperatures and occasional monsoon rains.

▶ **Accommodations:** Best Friends Roadhouse and Mercantile (435-644-3400; best friendsroadhouse.org) gets high ratings. Other dog-friendly options are highlighted at visitsouthernutah.com.

▶ **Supplies:** Best Friends Roadhouse and Mercantile has all your dog needs covered.

BURLINGTON

RECOMMENDED BY **Lyra Anderson**

Before arriving in Burlington, Lyra Anderson didn't realize the lengths that some towns would go to make their canine inhabitants feel at home. "I lived in Brattleboro, Vermont, before," she began, "and I didn't even know that such a thing as dog day care existed. I've been in Burlington since 2012, and I continue to be blown away by how much people here love their dogs. Sometimes it seems they love them more than their human children! People in Burlington desire the best for their dogs, and the city is responding with more parks and trails being made dog-friendly. It's cool to see how dogs can be included in so many aspects of human life."

Perched between Lake Champlain (America's sixth largest lake), bucolic dairy farms, and the ski slopes of nearby Stowe, the small city of Burlington (population approximately forty-five thousand in 2020) boasts a certain charm, with a downtown of cobblestone streets, a thriving university, and an unabashed hippie vibe. (If you doubt Burlington's counter-culture cred, recall that it is the home of Phish, Bernie Sanders, and Ben & Jerry's ice cream!) The abundance of locally raised meats and produce have fostered a thriving restaurant scene; brewers have likewise thrived, producing some of the most sought-after ales in North America. The proximity of mountains, rolling hills, wide-open fields, and Lake Champlain provide a great environment for canine companions.

A great place to begin your exploration of Burlington is the Church Street Marketplace district, a pedestrian-only area near the center of downtown. This collection of shops, restaurants, and pubs has been named one of America's Great Public Spaces by the American Planning Association. "Church Street is one of Burlington's biggest tourist attractions, and it's very inclusive to our four-legged friends," Lyra continued. "Walking down Church Street on a nice spring or summer day, you'll find more dogs than you can count. If you come out with a cute puppy, you'll have a tough time making your way down Church Street, as you'll be stopped fifty times. More and more of the restaurants are opening up patios so you can eat with your dog." One of the Church Street eateries that welcome dogs at outside tables is Ben & Jerry's (the site of the original Ben & Jerry's, in a renovated gas station, is just around the corner). Should a pint or two of Burlington's fine ale be in order, Lyra suggests the Vermont Pub & Brewery, Burlington's oldest brewpub, dating back to 1988: "They have a large outdoor seating area, so your dog won't feel like he's in a sardine can."

Should you and your dog seek a slightly less urban experience, there's no shortage of available trails. "I love exploring different hiking trails, and there are so many within the city limits that are accessible to dogs," Lyra said. One favorite is the Island Line Rail Trail, which skirts Lake Champlain for much of its thirteen-plus miles as it winds north to the town of Colchester. A bit farther north, Lyra likes Eagle Mountain Natural Area in the town of Milton. "There are trails through the woods, and wide-open fields that you and your dog can go romping through. If you hike up Eagle Mountain, you get great views of Lake Champlain and the Adirondack Mountains to the west." Another great romping ground a bit south of town is Shelburne Bay Park, where several paths near the lake await. "If I want to go further into the Green Mountains," Lyra added, "I just consult *50 Hikes in Vermont*." Most of the trails allow dogs on-leash."

Burlington's waterfront along Lake Champlain is extremely inviting—especially during the short but brilliant northern New England summers. "It's great to go to Waterfront Park," Lyra said. "There are lots of people laying out on blankets with their dogs, or playing Frisbee." If your dog would enjoy taking a swim, there are a few canine-friendly access points. One is Texaco Beach, which is not far north of the Waterfront Park dog park; another, Niquette Bay State Park, is in Colchester, the next town north. "Sections of the lake will sometimes get a summer algae bloom," Lyra described, "and it can be toxic for dogs. The city does a great job communicating conditions to the public so everyone can stay safe."

Catching a sunset with your pooch at one of the waterfront parks is a quintessential Burlington experience. As you're watching the sun dip below the Adirondacks, let your eyes return to the water—for Lake Champlain is said (by some) to be home to Champ, who some cryptozoologists have speculated to be a plesiosaur; others think the alleged creature could be a giant sturgeon. Like Nessie, the Loch Ness monster, Champ has been captured in fuzzy photographs and has been the subject of occasional tabloid-television coverage and rampant rumors. Port Henry, on the New York side of the lake, is said to be a favorite swimming ground of Champ. Even Samuel de Champlain, the French explorer from whom the lake gets its name, reported a sighting of such a creature more than four hundred years ago.

As a professional dog-handler, Lyra has many happy memories of sharing greater Burlington with her charges. She shared a favorite: "I care for a wonderful chocolate Lab named Jake, who's about ten years old. He loves tennis balls and he loves water—no surprise for a retriever! I'll often walk him on a trail that parallels Lake Champlain. Almost every time we take that trail, he'll be out in front of me, bounding along, and then suddenly he makes a ninety-degree beeline for the lake and takes a swim. I have to think that he's a happy dog, getting to hop in the lake almost anytime he wants. And I think that's what many dog owners enjoy about being in Burlington. It provides their animals the freedom to be a natural dog while still living in the city limits."

LYRA ANDERSON joined Play Dog Play as a part-time dog handler in 2012. Over the past ten years, she has played a role in every aspect of the company, from cleaning kennels to running the front desk to ordering retail for the Pine Street supply store. Lyra became part owner of Play Dog Play in 2016 and has been improving upon the company's approach to group socialization ever since. Her goal for Play Dog Play is to provide exceptional care for each dog on an individual level while meeting the needs of every dog on a large-scale social level. She feels that this is best accomplished when handlers take both the dog's physical needs and emotional needs into consideration. Lyra is the first to advocate that a day care environment should primarily be used for socialization and as a supplement to a dog's normal exercise routine. She's proud to have her company contribute positively and without judgment toward the quality of life each of our four-legged family members deserves. Lyra lives with her partner, daughter, and dog in Shelburne, where they can be found hiking around Vermont as much as possible or cheering New England sports teams to victory.

If You Go

▶ **Getting There:** Burlington International Airport is served by many major carriers.

▶ **Best Time to Visit:** Many love to visit Vermont in the early fall, prime "leaf-peeping" time . . . but late spring and summer can also be glorious.

▶ **Accommodations:** A number of Burlington hotels welcome dogs; see a list at bringfi-do.com. Made INN Vermont (802-399-2788; madeinnvermont.com), an eclectic bed-and-breakfast, gets high marks.

▶ **Supplies:** Pet Food Warehouse (pfwvt.com), with locations in South Burlington (802-862-5514) and Shelburne (802-985-3302), has all your supply needs covered . . . and they have wash stations, too, if your dog took a swim.

DESTINATION

48

WINTERGREEN

RECOMMENDED BY **Kim Salerno**

The area surrounding Charlottesville is known for its rustic, upscale vibe, hosting a number of boutique wineries, charming U-pick fruit orchards, and a robust farm-to-table dining scene. The city that houses Thomas Jefferson's famous Monticello estate is also nestled into the foothills of America's majestic Blue Ridge Mountains, making it a haven for outdoor recreation in the Appalachians.

"Charlottesville is a quaint little city in a big mountain valley," Kim Salerno began. "It's small, and yet there's so much going on. The go-to place is the downtown mall, but the name is a little deceptive. It has coffee shops and restaurants and boutiques and clubs, all in this big brick cobblestone walkway, covered by beautiful pin oak trees. There's always something going on. It's just loaded with outdoor seating, and most shops are super dog-friendly."

While you're downtown, be sure to pop into pet-friendly Mudhouse Specialty Coffee Roasters, or Three Notch'd Craft Kitchen & Brewery with their spacious outdoor seating area and complimentary dog bowls. Crate & Marrow is also worth a visit. "It's not your typical pet store," Kim explained. "The outside was designed to look like a Crate and Barrel, and they specialize in holistic, organic products. There's a nutritionist on-site you can chat with—overall, their staff is just crazy passionate and knowledgeable. You don't find a lot of places like this anymore."

There are a number of pet-friendly hotels in Charlottesville, but a particular favorite is Sonesta ES Suites. "It's close to the University of Virginia, so you're very central and can walk to just about anything," Kim said. "I have three big dogs, so having a suite was really nice to give everyone room. Not every hotel would be okay with that many dogs, but the staff was so welcoming; they did a phenomenal job hosting us."

Up in the mountains west of Charlottesville lies the little community of Wintergreen, a four-season paradise of natural splendor for those looking to escape the city. "If you love the outdoors, you have to go to Wintergreen. My parents were actually living in New Jersey at the time they heard about it, and started traveling there for weekend getaways," Kim said. "Eventually, the rest of the family heard the good word, and we started coming along, too. My parents ended up building a home there, and now the town feels like part of our family, just like our dogs."

Spring, summer, and fall are all great times to visit Wintergreen with your dog. Fall offers spectacular displays of color, and in the summer, the green stretches out for miles. "It's a hiker's heaven," Kim continued. "There are so many trails in the Blue Ridge Mountains, there's something for every person and dog, regardless of skill level. I do recommend trail maps, especially if you're new to the area, but you can basically show up to a trailhead, follow the sounds of the water, and before you know it, you'll be in this beautiful lush green paradise. It really is God's country."

The Nature Foundation at Wintergreen's website keeps a comprehensive list of hikes, organized by distance and difficulty. Some routes favored by dogs and families include Upper Shamokin Falls, a mile-long loop that meanders past streams, evergreen ferns, and wildflowers, and eventually ends at an impressive waterfall display. Another favorite is Chestnut Springs Trail, a two-mile out-and-back loop that's easy to moderate in difficulty. "It is so beautiful," described Kim. "You hike past streams and waterfalls, yellow birch trees, rhododendrons, and there are loads of wildflowers in the spring.

"A particular favorite of mine is the Claudius Crozet Blue Ridge Tunnel," she continued. "It's a railroad tunnel that runs through the mountain that was built between 1850 and 1858. It had been neglected, and was basically crumbled and caved in. Just within the last few years they renovated it, and opened it up to the community as a hiking trail. It's very long, and the inside is completely dark—you have to bring a flashlight. Water drips down; it's very eerie, a real walk into history. It takes us about fifteen minutes to get through to the other side."

Most trails in the Wintergreen area allow dogs to hike off-leash, so long as they are under voice control, but, Kim cautioned, "we always hike with leashes and horns on us, just in case you run into a bear that wants to say hello. Although we've never had any encounter like that."

OPPOSITE: The Blue Ridge Mountains around Wintergreen, North Carolina, are almost heaven for dog and human alike.

After working up an appetite, head down the mountain to the Basecamp Brewpub & Meadows. "They have a wonderful brewery there called Devils Backbone, but it's also a campground, a concert hall, and a restaurant," Kim enthused. "They have a massive, gorgeous outdoor seating area with big firepits, Adirondack chairs, and views of the mountain. You can hang outside with the dogs, grab a burger, chat with friends in the midst of this epic scenery. It's wonderful."

Although the eponymous Wintergreen Resort does not allow dogs, many other hotel and vacation properties in Nelson County do welcome pets. "In Nellysford, just a few miles from Wintergreen, there's an awesome B and B called the Mark Addy Inn. It's very unique, with eclectic décor, cute little rooms, and a gorgeous outdoor patio seating area with views of the mountains. They are the go-to B and B there if you have a dog." If you need a bit more space than a hotel room, the Wintergreen area has a rich condo- and home-rental market, and many welcome canine guests along with their owners.

Another hidden gem in the mountains east of Wintergreen is a small community known as Afton. "They have a great café there called Trager Brothers Coffee," Kim said. "I don't know about you, but I love my lattes. These guys have a few locations, and dogs are allowed inside. The setup is such that they have a big garage door that opens up the whole side of the building. The door opens, and boom—you see the mountains. Dogs are often playing in the field right next door; it's a beautiful site."

"If you want to get away and just shut off, Wintergreen is ideal," Kim concluded. "In Wintergreen, you're one with nature. After a day of adventuring, you can step out onto the deck, see the sunset, all the bright orange glow falling on the trees, glass of wine in your hand and your dog by your side. It doesn't get any better than that."

KIM SALERNO is the CEO and founder of TripsWithPets.com. Her love of animals, coupled with the need for a robust, no-nonsense pet-friendly hotel-booking site, was the motivation behind developing TripsWithPets. Kim has a great deal of personal experience traveling with her dogs, as well as with helping others plan trips with their pets. She strives to ensure pets are welcome, happy, and safe in their travels. In addition, Kim is a passionate animal advocate. She works very closely with pet rescue groups to help increase awareness and promote fostering. Further, Kim and her team raise funds for animal welfare 501(c)(3) organizations through TripsWithPets' annual Partners for

Animal Welfare Series (PAWS). Kim is a veteran of the online travel industry, and formerly oversaw digital marketing for New River Technologies, where she led marketing teams for both the Delta Air Lines and Continental Airlines Vacations websites.

If You Go

▶ **Getting There:** Charlottesville Albemarle Airport is served primarily by American (800-433-7300; aa.com), Delta (800-221-1212; delta.com), and United (800-864-8331; united.com). To get to Wintergreen, it's best to rent a car for the roughly thirty-five-mile scenic drive.

▶ **Best Time to Visit:** For hiking, outdoor eateries, and strolling the downtown mall, the best seasons are spring, summer, and fall. April and May see profusions of wildflowers, and fall foliage is famously beautiful.

▶ **Accommodations:** The Mark Addy in Nellysford (434-361-1101; mark-addy.com) takes year-round reservations . Sonesta ES Suites has a location Charlottesville (434-923-0300; sonesta.com). There is also a robust vacation home rental scene in Wintergreen.

▶ **Supplies:** Crate & Marrow (434-293-2275; crateandmarrow.com) is located in Charlottesville.

SEATTLE

RECOMMENDED BY **Cristina Ghiuzeli**

"Hendrix, my golden retriever, is a big dog who grew up in a big city," began Cristina. "He has a great disposition, but it was getting harder and hard to keep him cooped up inside all day in a small New York apartment. When we moved to Seattle, the landscape was completely different. There is so much more open space, more nature. And he loves it."

The West Coast's emerald city, snuggled in between the lofty Cascades to the east and the densely forested Olympics to the west, cultivates a notoriously nature-loving crowd. The elegant downtown houses upscale sports outfitters in the same storefront locations where other metropolises might put Cartier or Hermès. It comes as no surprise that man's best outdoor-adventure friend is welcome throughout the city.

"There are simply fewer restrictions," Cristina explained. "Lots of places have treats available at the ready for dogs, which makes sense, because everybody seems to have a dog here. You can bring your dog to any restaurant patio, of course, and a lot of coffee shops allow dogs inside, too."

Seattle is synonymous with a cup of well-brewed joe. Of the city's numerous notable cafés (including the original Starbucks), several welcome four-legged guests inside for a pup cup. Bark! Espresso, in the Northgate neighborhood, is a dog-themed café whose barista artists will paint your dog's face in the foam of your latte. Kaladi Brothers Coffee, just a mile up from the charming dockside markets at Pike Place, welcomes leashed dogs inside. A bit south and across the bridge in West Seattle, Ampersand Cafe on Alki serves up coffee, wine, made-in-house baked goods, and a lovely view of Alki Beach, and welcomes canine guests. (Keep in mind that to protect fragile marine animals, dogs are not allowed on saltwater beaches in Seattle—but this is just about the only wild area where they aren't permitted.)

OPPOSITE: Seattle's bustling Pike Place Market and numerous green parks welcome canines.

221

"Seattle has a lot of parks sprinkled throughout the city, and most of the time it's fine to be off-leash, as long as your dog is under voice control," Cristina continued. "My favorite is probably Discovery Park." On the city's west side, situated on Magnolia Bluff, Discovery Park offers spectacular views of the Olympic Mountains from dramatic sea cliffs overlooking the Puget Sound. The park's 524 acres of meadowland serve as a tranquil escape from the city, and an outdoor education resource site for its citizens, with streams, bluffs, trees, and grasslands.

In many cities, coifed and curated arboretums are the kind of parks that typically prohibit four-legged guests. Not the case in Seattle. The Washington Park Arboretum, whose botanical garden is curated by the University of Washington, welcomes dogs on-leash, allowing pets and humans to take in the sumptuous blooms and varied flora. "It's super walkable from the north end to the south end," described Cristina. "If you go in the fall, you'll find some bright orange and reds amongst the dark evergreens. In the spring, there are tons of camellias in bloom. It's a picturesque place to walk with your dog. There's also Magnuson Park, which is on the shore of Lake Washington and has a beautiful dog-friendly beach.

"My favorite memory with Hendrix, though, might be at Gas Works Park," Cristina continued. "You can go up to the top of the hill there, lay out a picnic, watch the waterplanes land in Lake Union, and see the Space Needle in the distance. The park has these big looping pipes and towers from the old power plant that were preserved after decommissioning. You can see so much of downtown Seattle. It's great to sit up there, above everything, watching the water and the city and the history, with Hendrix absorbing it all."

More open-space treats await you out of town. "If you feel like driving a bit," Cristina said, "Marymoor Park's off-leash dog park in Redmond is worth the visit. It's forty acres of pure off-leash park. There's a river dogs can swim in, crane birds come and visit . . . I've traveled a lot, and have never seen an off-leash park this big. And of course, because it's often rainy and they are running around, they get muddy. There are dog wash stations right there at the park to get them cleaned up before they get back in the car."

When it's time for chow, the Seattle Barkery serves up custom cookies, cakes, and even holiday-themed treats like Easter baskets for canine connoisseurs. You can also try to catch their Treat Truck, a food truck serving up freshly made gourmet dog treats, as it makes its rounds about town. "There's one neighborhood in particular that's super dog-friendly, which is Ballard," described Cristina. "There are tons of breweries, and they all have patios, usually with dogs already there by the time you show up. Urban Family Brewing Co. is my favorite, but around the corner there are, oh, about four or five others. And there are food trucks often parked outside that area. So you can basically walk around and brew-hop with your dog, eat some great food, and enjoy your evening without having to worry where you'll be welcome.

"One last thing—there are treats everywhere in Seattle," Cristina concluded. "Your dog is going to gain weight! But seriously, it is such a dog-friendly town. Whenever he goes, everyone comes up and says hello to Hendrix. Nobody is weird about bringing your dog anywhere. People love their dogs here, and they are almost universally respectful and playful. It's a great town for a dog to visit."

CRISTINA GHIUZELI is the proud mom of Hendrix, a rescued golden retriever trained as a therapy dog. As a working pup, he provides comfort to patients getting chemotherapy at a cancer center. Though raised in New York City, he now lives in Seattle, where his namesake, Jimi Hendrix, was from. As an extension of his work, he has an Instagram page, @hendrixthechelseagolden, where he provides a daily dose of happiness to a broader audience. On their Instagram channel, Cristina and Hendrix share pictures of their adventures and their favorite cafés, parks, art, and more. Even on rainy, cloudy days of Seattle winter, Hendrix's smile shines through.

If You Go

▶ **Getting There:** Seattle is served by many carriers, and is the hub of Alaska Airlines (800-252-7522; alaskaair.com).
▶ **Best Time to Visit:** Summers are clear and temperate, and the days are long. Seattle has notoriously rainy winters.
▶ **Accommodations:** Visit Seattle lists a variety of dog-friendly hotels and rentals at visit seattle.com.
▶ **Supplies:** Seattle has dozens of pet supply shops, but Mud Bay (www.mudbay.com) is a favorite local chain for holistic foods and high quality gear. There are handful of locations around the city and in neighboring counties.

Library of Congress Control Number: 2022946067

ISBN: 978-1-4197-6100-3
eISBN: 978-1-64700-638-9

Photograph credits: Page(s) 2: Tripp Fay Photography; 8: Gabrielle Chan Attong @thecitycanines; 12, 22: EyeEm/Alamy Stock Photo; 16: RossHelen editorial/Alamy Stock Photo; 18: Laura George; 30: Irene McHugh; 34: Shandos Cleaver; 38: Amanda Klecker @jonathanwarrenofficial; 42: Zjerome Photography; 46: Sarah Mickel; 52: Edgar Bullon/Alamy Stock Photo; 58: Cori Godfrey; 62: Jenna Murray of Spilled Milk Creative; 66: Allison Shamrell Pet Photography; 74: Blue Amrich; 78: Cavan Images/Alamy Stock Photo; 84: Michael Ryno Photography; 88: Jaromír Chalabala/Alamy Stock Photo; 92: Melissa Halliburton/BringFido; 98: Alexandra Fitzgerald, Dog Photographer of Tampa Bay; 104: Tayler Green; 108: Lindsey Tom; 112: Luiza Puiu Photography; 116: Doggy's Island Resort and Villa (Japan); 120: Michael Carni/Shutterstock; 126: Mercedes Mehling/Shutterstock; 132: Dr. Laurie Coger, Healthy Dog Workshop; 138: Kevin Judd Photography; 142: Explore Asheville; 150: Ruffwear; 154: Roby Babcock; 158: Anna Christian; 168: Mai Tran/Herky the Cavalier; 172: Ashlyn George/The Lost Girl's Guide to Finding the World; 180: National Parks Board, Singapore; 184: @remyaroundtheworld; 188: Kristel Segeren/The Tiny Travelogue; 192: @goldenguycoop; 196: Glenn Ruthven/Alamy Stock Photo; 202: Nakhon Sawan/Shutterstock; 206: Parker Moore; 216: Glenna Martin; 220: Kim Hương Trần (littlecooperbear)

Jacket © 2023 Abrams

Editors: Samantha Weiner and Juliet Dore
Designer: Anna Christian
Design Manager: Danny Maloney
Managing Editor: Annalea Manalili
Production Manager: Kathleen Gaffney

This book was composed in Interstate, Scala, and Village.

Printed and bound in China
10 9 8 7 6 5 4 3 2 1

ABRAMS The Art of Books
195 Broadway, New York, NY 10007
abramsbooks.com